There is much rhetoric in education around the role of peer c(*standing of how to make coaching effective. Dr. Foltos has be.* *movement with more than a decade of experience working in over 40 countries to build communities of professional learners supporting each other.* Peer Coaching: Unlocking the Power of Collaboration *draws on this experience to provide a detailed topography of why teacher professional learning through peer coaching is so important in enabling teachers as partners in improving learning for students. At the core is a simple message, working together on improving teaching and learning in a supportive environment makes a big difference for children. The book explains in detail the how to make this work!*

Greg Butler, Senior Director
Education Strategic Partnership

The insights and ideas in this book work in many ways as a guide for the school leader and peer who wants to build a climate of sharing and collaboration built on trust and reflection. Based on his vast experience, research, and empathy Les Foltos shows anyone involved in education the path to future learning environments.

Mike Hellgren, Teacher and Peer Coach

Dr. Les Foltos offers a wonderful insight into the theoretical world of peer coaching as well as invaluable practical lessons gained from many years of observing and supporting teachers across the globe. I thoroughly recommend this book to anyone with a passion for collaborating with colleagues to improve the future of their students.

Christine Simmons
Master Trainer, Executive Coach

The book explains in words what every teacher and school leader should already be considering: how to prepare our students for the coming century by collaborating, sharing, and using technology as a powerful tool.

Jerker Porat, Teacher and Peer Coach

Peer Coaching: Unlocking the Power of Collaboration *will be a useful tool for any district undertaking the development of a peer coaching program. The future of education rests on collaboration among teachers to provide the best learning activities and embedded technology for students, and peer coaching provides the vehicle that will allow that collaboration to be effective.*

Kay Teehan, Technology Resource Specialist
Polk County Schools

In this book, Les Foltos presents an outstanding and practical case for schools to develop staff by utilizing peer coaching. As a result, today's students will learn the 21st century skills they will need for the future.

Dr. Linda Gross Cheliotes, School Leadership Coach
Coaching For Results Global

This book narrows in on an important concept: people discuss the importance of collaboration, but successful collaboration is rarely defined. Through Peer Coaching, *Les Foltos analyzes factors and processes of how to develop innovative, coherent, educational instruction, with student learning central to its focus.*

Maria Muzzo, K–8 Teacher and PhD candidate in Education,
University of Washington

*To my children, Jack and Greta, whose support
and patience made this possible.*

Peer Coaching

Unlocking the Power of Collaboration

Les Foltos

CORWIN
A SAGE Company

CORWIN
A SAGE Company

FOR INFORMATION

Corwin
A SAGE Company
2455 Teller Road
Thousand Oaks, California 91320
(800) 233-9936
www.corwin.com

SAGE Ltd.
1 Oliver's Yard
55 City Road
London, EC1Y 1SP
United Kingdom

SAGE Pvt. Ltd.
B 1/I 1 Mohan Cooperative Industrial Area
Mathura Road, New Delhi 110 044
India

SAGE Publications Asia-Pacific Pte. Ltd.
3 Church Street
#10–04 Samsung Hub
Singapore 049483

Acquisitions Editor: Arnis Burvikovs
Associate Editor: Desirée A. Bartlett
Editorial Assistants: Mayan White and Ariel Price
Permissions Editor: Jennifer Barron
Project Editor: Veronica Stapleton Hooper
Copy Editor: Kim Husband
Typesetter: Hurix Systems Private Ltd.
Proofreader: Sarah J. Duffy
Indexer: Sheila Bodell
Cover Designer: Anupama Krishnan

Printed in the United States of America

A catalog record of this book is available from the Library of Congress.

ISBN: 9781452257341

This book is printed on acid-free paper.

Certified Chain of Custody
SUSTAINABLE FORESTRY INITIATIVE
Promoting Sustainable Forestry
www.sfiprogram.org
SFI-01268

SFI label applies to text stock

13 14 15 16 17 10 9 8 7 6 5 4 3 2 1

Contents

Preface xi

Acknowledgments xvii

About the Author xxi

Chapter 1: Coaching Roles and Responsibilities 1

 Coaching: Getting Started 3
  Coaching Roles 4
  Understanding the Environment for Coaching 6
 Defining the Coaching Relationship 8
  Friendly 8
  Personalized 10
  Manageable 11
  Private 14
  Supported 14
 Relationships, Respect, and Trust 16
  Expert vs. Trust 18
  How Coaches Carry Out Roles 20
 Summary 22

Chapter 2: Why Peer Coaching? 23

 Professional Development: Wishful Thinking 25
 Professional Learning That Works 27
  Improving Practice Can Only Be
  Done by Teachers, Not to Teachers 27

Characteristics of Effective Professional
Development   29
Highly Collaborative   29
Intensive and Ongoing   30
On the Job, Connected to Classroom Practice   31
Peer Coaching and Effective
Professional Learning   32
Peer Coaches' Effectiveness   34
Riding the Wave of the Ripple Effect   34
Washington State: Enhanced Peer Coaching   35
Wisconsin's Peer Coaching Collaborative   36
Summary   37

Chapter 3: Preparing Coaches   39

Who Coaches and Why?   40
From Teacher Leader to Coach: What Do Peer
Coaches Need to Know?   43
Coaching Skills: Communication
and Collaboration Skills   45
Lesson Design   47
ICT Integration   49
Content-Specific Training?   51
Peer Coach Training at a Glance   52
Highly Collaborative   53
Connected to Classroom Practice   53
Intensive, Sustained   54
Summary   55

Chapter 4: The Coaching Plan   57

Is Coaching Right for Your School?   59
Creating the Coaching Plan   60
Elements of the Coaching Plan   61
Academic Focus   61
Collaborating Teachers   61
Three Models for Choosing a Collaborating Teacher   63
Coach Roles and Responsibilities   65
Norms   65
Resources   66
Communication   68
Aligning Professional-Development Efforts   71

Measuring Progress   72
Coaching Plan: Next Steps   73
Building Capacity: Bringing Coaching to Scale   73
Summary   76

Chapter 5: Communication and Collaboration   77

Collaboration Needs to Be "...structured,
taught, and learned"   79
Meeting Norms   79
Collaborative Norms   81
Communication Skills   83
Active Listening   83
Paraphrasing   84
Clarifying Questions   85
Probing Questions   85
Inquiry Over Advocacy   87
Developing Communication
and Collaboration Skills   88
Conducting a Planning Meeting   88
Moving From Nice to Innovation   89
Removing the Fear Factor   91
Safety Net   93
Small Changes: Continuous Improvement   93
Recognition   94
Model Risk Taking   95
Challenging Probing Questions   95
Summary   99

Chapter 6: Defining Effective Learning Activities   101

Characteristics of Effective Learning   104
Norm for Effective Learning   109
Assess Lesson Design   113
Start Positive   115
Start Small   116
Summary   118

Chapter 7: Lesson-Improvement Process   119

Create a Task   122
Define Standards   124
Learning Context   125

Student Directions   126
Reflection and Feedback   128
Assessment   129
Resources   131
Summary   132

Chapter 8: Enhancing Learning by Integrating
Technology   **133**

Coaching: Linking Learning and Technology   135
Test Scores and Technology Integration   139
It's Not About the Technology,
    It's About the Learning   141
    Technology as Play-Doh   141
    Transforming Traditional Teaching and Learning? 142
    Supporting and Enhancing 21st-Century Learning 143
    Pedagogy Needs to Drive Technology Use 145
Technology Integration Redefined   146
    Coaching Teachers to Integrate Technology 147
Peer Coaching Technology Integration Toolkit   149
    Lesson-Improvement Process   150
    Peeling the Onion   150
    Emphasizing Student Tasks   151
Summary   151

Chapter 9: Connecting Coaching Skills to Practice   **153**

Learning From Successes and Challenges   154
    Collaboration to Improve Learning 156
Observation   158
    Focus on the Learners   158
    Preobservation Meetings   160
Effective Reflection   161
    Collaborative Norms   161
    Video and Observation   162
    The Power of Protocols   162
    Feedback   163
Ongoing Professional Learning   164
Summary   167

**Chapter 10: Sustaining Coaching
and Building Capacity**   **169**

   Implementing Peer Coaching: The Basics   170
     Peer Coaching: Expense vs. Investment   171
   Building Support to Build Capacity   172
     School Leadership   172
     Communicating About Coaching   174
     Vision Building   174
   **Building Capacity to Improve Teaching
   and Learning and Build Support**   176
     More Peer Coaches   176
     Creating a Norm for Effective Learning 177
     *Peer Coaches and Professional Learning
     Communities*   179
   Peer Coaching and Culture   180
   "It's a System Thing, Not a Single Thing" 181
     *Edmonds School District's Peer
     Coaching Experience*   182
     Peer Coaching in Flagstaff   183
     Apache Junction and Peer Coaching   184
   Summary   187
   Final Thoughts   187

References   **191**
Index   **199**

Preface

The idea to train peer coaches grew out of my search for strategies that would help teachers improve teaching and learning. Research and experience have shown that collaboration among teachers is the key toward this endeavor.

The early efforts I led at collaborative professional learning helped teachers improve their practice, but what they learned rarely spread beyond their classrooms. Spreading innovative practices across a school seemed to require some sort of key to unlock the power of collaboration. Schools needed teacher leaders to lead collaborative professional learning in their schools. Peer Coaches could be that key.

Four nucleotides make up the DNA of Peer Coaching. The first is the fact that **effective professional learning results from collaborating with a peer**, someone teachers know and respect and who is just down the hall to help when needed. The second is the belief that **collaboration is more successful if one of the peers is a Peer Coach** who is highly skilled in communication, collaboration, lesson design, and integrating technology. Third, **successful coaches need a willing, engaged learning partner.** Finally, if we want to avoid creating more small-scale, short-lived educational experiments, **coaching needs to be part of a plan that aligns coaching with the school's goals** and provides the support the Peer Coach and her or his learning partner need for success.

Today, in more than 40 countries, teachers who collaborate with a Peer Coach report that their Peer Coach provides a safety net that encourages them to take risks to improve teaching and learning. Working with a Peer Coach, they are engaged in a process of continuous improvement designed to help their students learn the basics and 21st-century skills. Peer Coaches have demonstrated that they are effective at unlocking the power of collaboration to improve teaching and learning (Ley, 2011; Liston & Ragan, 2010).

How Will This Book Help You?

This book blends theory, the research behind coaching, and practice. Its unique strength comes from the practical experiences shared by dozens of highly successful Peer Coaches from the United States and across the world. Their shared experiences offer invaluable guidance and advice that will help coaches succeed. The book also features resources drawn from Peer Coach training activities that will be valuable to anyone interested in coaching. Some of these include a template for creating a Coaching Plan, the Learning Activity Checklist, a research-based tool that defines the qualities of highly effective learning, and a step-by-step lesson-improvement process used by coaches and their learning partners to translate the checklist into effective classroom learning. In addition, the book draws on my experiences helping educators implement coaching in hundreds of school districts around the world, experiences that provide rich resources that will guide coaches and school leaders to implement coaching successfully.

WHO SHOULD USE THIS BOOK

The book is designed for educators who believe the future of education depends on effective collaboration among teachers to improve teaching and learning. It addresses a variety of issues school leaders face as they implement a coaching program to improve teaching and learning. Teacher leaders who are moving into coaching roles will find the book provides a wealth of practical insights into strategies for effective coaching.

Educators New to Coaching

I hope the book encourages educators who are considering coaching to adopt it and provides insights and resources vital to implementing a successful Peer Coaching program for those educators just launching one. For example, it defines the attributes of successful coaches to help schools make wise choices as they select Peer Coaches and offers proven strategies for selecting teachers to collaborate with coaches. The book provides an understanding of the roles Peer Coaches and their collaborating teachers play. Successful coaching is far more difficult than having one peer offer advice to another, and the book provides advice from successful coaches on strategies and skills they have used. Finally, this work is designed to provide prospective Peer Coaches and school leaders with ideas on how to align peer coaching with school goals and how to support and sustain coaching successfully.

Experienced Educators

The book is also designed for principals, coaches, and educators in schools that already have coaching programs and are looking for ways to make coaching more effective. While the book emphasizes one type of Peer Coaching, much of what makes these Peer Coaches successful is immediately relevant to any coach focused on improving teaching and learning. The issues I address throughout the book, like building trust, using communication skills to build a safety net, and emphasizing inquiry to build capacity to improve student learning, have value for any educator involved in coaching. Schools involved in coaching should benefit from my materials on how schools and districts can successfully support and sustain coaching. In addition, the book offers valuable insights into how to use coaching to produce systemic improvement in teaching and learning.

BOOK AT A GLANCE

Chapter 1 explains the roles Peer Coaches assume and how they play these roles to create a relationship based on respect and trust. It also explores strategies coaches can use to build this kind of relationship with their collaborating teachers.

Chapter 2 examines the research about the strategies that are most likely to improve student learning, research on effective professional learning, and how Peer Coaching aligns with both fields of research.

Chapter 3 defines three critical coaching skills, communication and collaboration skills, lesson-design skills, and technology integration and outlines why these skills are essential to build the coach's capacity to assist other teachers to improve instruction.

Chapter 4 outlines a step-by-step look at the elements of a Coaching Plan designed to align coaching with the school's goals and make Peer Coaching effective. It also explores how school leaders can use the planning process as part of their overall strategy to build their schools' collective capacity to improve teaching and learning.

Chapter 5 offers insight into communication and collaboration skills Peer Coaches need to be successful. It also provides insights into how Peer Coaches use these skills to create a safety net that encourages their collaborating teachers to take risks and improve teaching and learning.

Chapter 6 examines the importance of creating a norm for effective learning for successful Peer Coaching and the broader success of schoolwide improvement of teaching and learning. It also provides practical insights into how Peer Coaches can use this norm to assist peers in the ongoing process of improving teaching and learning.

Chapter 7 gives educators a structured lesson-improvement process and related resources that coaches and their collaborating teachers have successfully used to improve learning activities to help students develop basic skills and 21st-century skills.

Chapter 8 provides insights into the ways Peer Coaches use learning tasks like communication or collaboration as the starting points for integrating technology and offers other key approaches coaches use to ensure that teachers use technology to enhance 21st-century learning.

Chapter 9 explores the ongoing development of coaches after they have gained some on-the-job coaching experiences. It examines the strategies and tools coaches can use to shape structured discussions about successes and challenges they face and their use of protocols to foster safe, focused reflective discussions after observing a peer.

Chapter 10 provides insights into strategies successful Peer Coaches have used to build support for coaching within the school and how these efforts can align with school and school district efforts to create capacity to improve teaching and learning.

I have been constantly amazed at the ways these dedicated and skillful professionals have helped peers to improve teaching and learning. I hope this book encourages schools to rely on Peer Coaching to unlock the power of collaboration to improve teaching and learning in their schools.

Acknowledgments

Many people contributed to *Peer Coaching: Unlocking the Power of Collaboration.* Karen Meyer, Karen Peterson, and I shaped the initial curriculum and implementation model for Peer Coaching while we worked together at a non-profit now known as the Edlab Group. Karen Meyer took the lead in drafting much of the curriculum we use to prepare coaches. Over the past 20 years, she has also taught me the value of collaboration and what it takes to make collaboration between teachers effective. Karen Peterson provided badly needed organizational skills to bring the curriculum together and brought those same skills to our efforts to implement and assess the Peer Coaching program. Eeva Reeder joined the three of us at crucial points and provided critical ideas on the attributes of highly effective teaching and learning. Without them, Peer Coaching wouldn't exist. Mike McMann, Vicky Ragan, Shelee King-George, and Matt Huston joined us at various stages along the way and helped partners around the world to implement Peer Coaching. They drew on these experiences to revise and improve Peer Coaching in ways that better met the needs of educators. In addition, I learned a great deal from each of them and hope some small part of that learning is reflected here.

Late in 2003, Greg Butler recognized the value of collaboration for educators and gave us the opportunity to make Peer Coaching part of Microsoft's new Partners in Learning program. He opened the door to expand Peer Coaching beyond Washington State. Ana Teresa Ralston immediately recognized the value of Peer Coaching and led Brazil to become the first country to implement Peer Coaching. Her ideas and support gave me the confidence to encourage other countries to adopt Peer Coaching. Since then, more than 40 countries have adopted and implemented Peer Coaching. David Walddon also understood the value coaches could play in improving teaching and learning and championed Peer Coaching throughout his tenure in Microsoft's Partners in Learning program. Their support gave me the chance to work with thousands of educators from around the world and provided the learning opportunities that made this book possible.

Many educators provided direct assistance as I wrote this book. Over the years, hundreds of Peer Coaches and the teachers they have collaborated with have shared their experiences with me. More than 100 Peer Coaches from eight countries were willing to endure my interviewing skills and share what they learned from their experiences. Mary Knight, Mary Lou Ley, Kim Mathey, and Tracy Watanabe repeatedly offered me extensive insights into the successes and challenges they faced as they implemented Peer Coaching. Without the experiences of each of these educators who were willing to share their learning, this book would be nothing but theory. Norm Lee and Eva Pethrus both offered a different kind of support. Each repeatedly encouraged me to write this book because they felt educators would benefit. I needed that push.

Maria Muzzo, Bryce Nelson, Chris Simmons, Karen Soine, and David Walddon read each of the chapters and offered critical insights into how to improve the text. Julie Lorton and Karen Meyer also read some sections of the text and shared their wisdom and expertise. The book is much stronger as a result of the contributions each of them made. Any weaknesses are a result of my failure to listen to their advice more closely.

Publisher's Acknowledgments

Corwin wishes to acknowledge the following peer reviewers for their editorial insight and guidance.

Dr. Linda Gross Cheliotes, School Leadership Coach
Coaching For Results Global
Hoyt, KS

Maria Muzzo, K–8 Teacher and PhD candidate in Education,
University of Washington
Seattle, WA

Dr. Marceta Fleming Reilly, Leadership Coach,
    Corwin Author
Coaching For Results Global
Hoyt, KS

Kay Teehan, Technology Resource Specialist
Polk County Schools
Lakeland, FL

Dr. Claudia Thompson
Academic Officer, Learning and Teaching
Peninsula School District

About the Author

 **Les Foltos** started his career in education as a history teacher and unexpectedly found himself leading the instructional technology program for Seattle Public Schools through its first widespread efforts to integrate technology into the classroom. In that role, he came face to face with the need to develop and use more effective strategies for professional learning. Success with early efforts to make professional learning highly collaborative led to his initial experiments with coaching.

Since 2001, Foltos has been involved in Peer Coaching. He led the team that created the Peer Coaching program that helps teacher leaders to develop the skills they need to coach colleagues to improve teaching and learning. Since 2004, when Microsoft made Peer Coaching a part of its Partners in Learning program, Foltos has helped educators across the United States and in more than 40 other countries adopt and implement Peer Coaching.

Foltos is currently the director of Peer-Ed and continues to work with educators to develop the skills they need to collaborate with peers and improve teaching and learning in ways that meet the needs of their students. He is a co-author of ISTE's *Coaching White Paper*. Foltos is also a frequent speaker at national and international conferences, including a TEDx presentation in 2011.

1

Coaching Roles and Responsibilities

I never teach my pupils. I only attempt to provide the conditions in which they can learn.

—Albert Einstein

There is nearly universal acceptance today that schools need to change. Our K–12 educational system has always been shaped by our economic and social needs. Unfortunately, Sir Ken Robinson observed, "The current [educational] system was designed and conceived for a different age" (Robinson, 2010). Most of us no longer work in manufacturing or on the farm as we did just one generation ago. Today we work in a service-based economy in which the success of companies like Amazon.com is driven by a "chief logarithmic officer." For most of us, this is hard to imagine. Logarithms were one more aspect of math class that convinced us that math had no meaning beyond high school. Now they drive innovation. Our life beyond work has also been transformed. Technology has changed how we communicate, access information, buy products and services, and even entertain ourselves. Who would have imagined just 10 years ago that a film about a guy who created a social networking app would be a Best Picture nominee for an Academy Award? Until quite recently, my social network was defined by how many people "liked" my Christmas card and sent one back.

Responding to these changing circumstances, business and political leaders in countries around the world have defined the skills they need and want from education. Educational and business leaders agree that there is a consistent set of skills students need to master to be successful in today's changing workplace. The Partnership for 21st Century Skills, a group made up of American business and educational leaders, reflects many ideas commonly held by leaders around the world. These policy makers insist that students must develop skills in the four Cs:

> These policy makers who define the skills students need insist that students must develop skills in the four Cs:
>
> - critical thinking
> - communication
> - collaboration
> - creativity

- critical thinking
- communication
- collaboration
- creativity (Partnership for 21st Century Skills, n.d.)

Based on my conversations with thousands of educators from more than 50 countries around the world, it is clear to me that educators agree. When I have asked them to define the skills and competencies their students need for success, their lists always include the four Cs.

Most of these same educators believe that traditional education will not prepare students with those critical skills. Researchers agree. Richard Elmore (2004) found that in far too many classrooms today, student learning emphasizes repetition and memorization; assessment typically asks students to repeat what they learned from the teacher or text by completing tests that stress recall and recognition. Educators and policy makers from across the United States banded together to create the Common Core State Standards, at least in part because of the growing consensus that traditional education was not preparing students with the kinds of skills they need for success. Even a cursory reading of the Common Core State Standards should make it clear that the authors of these standards believe there is a need for fundamental improvement in teaching and learning in ways that would help students develop 21st-century skills.

So here is the $64,000 question: What do schools need to do if they hope to improve teaching and learning to meet students' needs? For more than a decade, I have found that Peer Coaches can play a critical role in helping teachers improve student learning. Coaches aren't the whole answer, but they are an important part of the answer.

COACHING: GETTING STARTED

In its simplest terms, Peer Coaching is one teacher helping another to improve. A Peer Coach is a teacher leader who assists a peer to improve standards-based instruction by supporting the peer's efforts to actively engage students in 21st-century learning activities. Coaches help colleagues improve teaching and learning by assisting them to develop the necessary lesson-design skills and instructional and technology integration strategies needed to prepare their students for college and careers.

Coaching is certainly not a new idea. Athletes, professional singers, and business executives have long used coaches. For educators, coaching has much

> Coaching is certainly not a new idea. Athletes, professional singers, and business executives have long used coaches. For educators, coaching has much deeper roots. The methodology dates back at least to Socrates more than 2,500 years ago.

deeper roots. The methodology dates back at least to Socrates more than 2,500 years ago. It is familiar to teachers. When prospective coaches learn about the roles Peer Coaches play, they insist that they have coached others. As one Peer Coach noted, "Peer Coaching helped give a formal name to things we're already doing, and gave us permission to do these activities" (T. Calsyn, personal communication, September 8, 2011).

While the idea behind coaching is old and the concept of coaching is easy to understand, there is nothing simple about being an effective coach. To explore how complex the task of coaching is, let's try to answer a question a brand-new coach raised just after she had completed the training designed to help her develop coaching skills. She was stuck and asked me, "How do I get started coaching?" What she really wanted to know was:

- What roles should I play?
- As my relationship with my peers develops, when will it be appropriate for me to play roles like expert or catalyst?
- How do I play these roles?

Coaching Roles

If a coach expects to be successful at helping another teacher improve student learning, the coach needs a clear idea of what roles he or she will play before beginning coaching. The list of potential roles a coach might play is extensive, but a handful are key. Coaches help colleagues by:

- **Providing just-in-time training or resources** (Meyer et al., 2011d). Teachers may want their coach to help them find a great resource for a learning activity they are planning. For example, they might need a resource for an activity that asks students how to preserve a rainforest. Or they may want a bit of training on how to set up a SkyDrive so their students can more easily collaborate on a forest-preservation project with students in others countries.

- **Coplanning learning activities** (Meyer et al. 2011d). Teachers who collaborate with coaches often want to sit down for more in-depth planning. They may want a coach's assistance in revising an existing activity on preserving forests to emphasize problem solving, to engage students in assessing their own work, to recast the activity so it has more meaning to the students' lives outside of school, or to use technology so the students can share their work with the community and get feedback.
- **Modeling or team teaching to demonstrate effective teaching and reflection afterward** (Meyer et al., 2011d). I have found that teachers from all of the 50 countries that I have worked with want to see what strong teaching looks like. In fact, teachers who work with coaches often say this is the most effective form of coaching. To see strong teaching in practice, the teacher may watch the coach teach, or the coach and teacher may team-teach. Modeling is more than just showing. Typically the teacher and coach may meet before the classroom visit to define what they will be focusing on in the classroom and in their discussion after this observation. The reflection after the observation gives the teacher and coach an opportunity to discuss what occurred, how the collaborating teacher might adopt these ideas, and what kind of support the teacher might need from the coach as they adopt this practice.
- **Observing teachers and reflecting on what they observed** (Meyer et al. 2011d). At some point in the coaching relationship, after trust is established, teachers will ask their coach to observe them in their classrooms. In the reflection that follows the observation, it is important to define what worked and why it worked in order to discuss how the teacher could use what worked in other

> This process of observation and reflection is the most effective form of formative assessment for educators. It is their key to life-long learning.

learning activities. These reflections also include what the teacher being observed might do differently next time. This process of observation and reflection is the most effective form of formative assessment for educators. It is their key to life-long learning.

- **Playing no role in teacher evaluation.** As we will see shortly, coaching rests entirely on building a relationship of trust between the coach and the teachers who collaborate with the coach. Nothing would destroy trust faster than having coaches evaluate their peers. A *New Yorker* article on coaching really puts the coach's role in perspective: "The allegiance of coaches is to the people they work with: their success depends on it" (Gawande, 2011).

Peer Coaches quickly grasp the roles they need to play, but before coaches begin coaching, they need to have some understanding of the environment they will be working in.

Understanding the Environment for Coaching

Two-thirds of teachers and three-quarters of principals told researchers in a Met Life survey that they believed that greater collaboration "would have a major impact on improving student achievement" (Markow & Pieters, 2010, p. 11). Reading the summary of this survey could lead prospective coaches to believe that American educators understood the value of collaboration and were acting on that belief. If they drew this conclusion, they would be wrong. While most educators intuitively recognize the value of collaboration, working in isolation is still largely the norm in American schools (Darling-Hammond, Wei, Andree, Richardson, & Orphanos, 2009; Markow & Peters, 2010; Mirel & Goldin, 2012).

This conclusion may seem a bit confusing if you enter almost any school at the start of the day; you will find educators asking each other about birthday celebrations, movies, or a recent sports event. In fact, they will talk about almost anything but the craft of teaching. Despite these signs of personal friendship, there is little professional collaboration.

When I ask coaches to describe collaboration in their schools, many tell me that teachers work alone behind closed doors, and there isn't much collaboration when they come out of their rooms. For many teachers, photocopying and sharing common activities were the limit of collaboration and coplanning. Many coaches' comments echoed those of Melanie Hogan, an Australian Peer Coach, who observed that if you asked for help in her school, there were people willing to help. But for the most part, "People got on with their task in their classroom" (M. Hogan, personal communication, July 13, 2011). Let's not blame the teachers. Working in isolation is a by-product of their schools and school systems. In a study of professional learning, former Governor James Hunt concluded that schools use an "outmoded factory model of school organization," which produces "egg crate isolation" for teachers (Darling-Hammond et al., 2009, p. 2). Rephrased slightly, Hunt argues that schools still use a production-line model of education in which individuals work in isolation to perform their part in assembling their product: students.

Fear Factor is a TV show that asks participants to take incredible risks and do things that frighten most of us so badly that we could not imagine doing them. Any coach who is just getting started needs to understand that there is little in the culture of most schools that supports collaboration, risk taking, or innovation. One fear factor that makes American teachers uncomfortable can be defined in four simple letters: NCLB (No Child Left Behind). Virtually every American educator understands that NCLB means student test scores must go up every year or the school will be branded a failure. More recently, teachers are concerned that the high-stakes standardized tests spawned by NCLB will be used to brand individual teachers as successes or failures. The Race to the Top program has put more pressure on school systems to adopt new systems of evaluating teachers and added another fear factor. Teachers worry that standardized test data from high-stakes tests will be the centerpiece school systems use to reward the successful teachers and deal with those who aren't successful. It is not an environment that encourages risk taking.

Coaches also need to understand that for many educators, working with a Peer Coach, who asks the peer to take risks as they collaborate to improve the teacher's lessons and invite the coach

> Many teachers might define their fear factor as a Peer Coach who asks them to take risks and perhaps fail.

to observe the teacher at work, is like asking that educator to be a participant on *Fear Factor*. What the coach's learning partner hears is, "My coach is asking me to open the doors of my classroom and to demonstrate what I know and what I don't know. My coach is asking me to take risks and make mistakes in public." As one Peer Coach, Jennie Warmouth, noted, it is "hard to be willing to make mistakes in front of others, because it will be so hard to overcome this perceived failure" (J. Warmouth, personal communication, September 7, 14, 2011). Many teachers might define their fear factor as a Peer Coach who asks them to take risks and perhaps fail. Fortunately, these are challenges that a coach can address and minimize by understanding what makes a relationship with a collaborating teacher work.

DEFINING THE COACHING RELATIONSHIP

Pauline Hunt, a Peer Coach in one of Sydney's suburbs, told me that as she begins collaborating with a learning partner, she wants that teacher to understand that their relationship will be defined by five words: *friendly, personalized, manageable, private,* and *supported* (P. Hunt, personal communication, June 29, 2012). While other Peer Coaches have not been quite as succinct in defining the factors that shape a coach's success, most Peer Coaches agree that these five words are critical to successful coaching. Let's take a closer look at how each of those words defines the coaching relationship and makes it successful.

Friendly

Anyone with a career understands that friendship comes in two flavors: personal and professional. Peer Coaches will tell you that having a personal friendship with a learning partner is important; having a professional friendship is essential. Peer Coaches often talk about the importance of using emotional intelligence or people skills. If a coach is using these skills, he or she understands that his or her colleagues must feel comfortable in the relationship if they want the relationship to be productive. Tracy Watanabe, a Peer Coach from Arizona, told prospective coaches that it "takes time and energy to build those relationships," she insisted, "but it is the key in coaching" (Watanabe, 2011). Successful Peer Coaches from around the world have told me exactly the same thing: Without rapport and a strong relationship, coaches won't be effective. In these same conversations, coaches described a variety of strategies to create these friendly relationships.

When many coaches meet with a collaborating teacher for the first time, they make a point of asking how the teacher is and asking about other educators or friends both know. This discussion might go on for 20 to 30 minutes before they get to anything related to teaching or coaching. These coaches are making a point of ensuring that their peers are comfortable. Other coaches who use the same strategy report that their initial conversations with peers occur over coffee, treats, or lunch.

Another key to building a friendly relationship, successful Peer Coaches believe, is to make it clear to their learning partners that they are true peers. Coaches repeatedly say that when they collaborate with another teacher, they work hard to prove they are equals who want to work and learn together to improve teaching and learning. Anna Walter, an experienced Peer Coach, insists, "You must present yourself as a peer, I am a teacher, you are a teacher and we are working together on a level playing field (A. Walter, personal communication, September 28, 2011). Knight's (2011a) research on coaching led him to agree that having both partners share ideas and make decisions as equals is essential to a successful partnership.

Peer Coaches insist that establishing their relationship as peers requires that they create a respectful relationship with their learning partners. Experienced Peer Coaches understand that one way to show respect to their peers is to learn with and from them. Paul Shanahan, one of the first Peer Coaches, says that learning is "always a two-way street. The coach always needs to make it clear [to their peer] that this is symbiotic, and [the coach] is always learning something from you" (P. Shanahan, personal communication, September 6, 2011). In other words, the coach needs to show respect to get respect. Successful Peer Coaches endorse this same concept. Some of them have told me that they try to be explicit about what they are learning from their collaborating teacher and how they use it. Other coaches also work hard to create opportunities for their learning partners to help them. In his article *What Good Coaches Do*, Jim Knight (2011b), agrees that this kind of colearning, which he calls reciprocity, is a part of a successful coaching partnership. Demonstrating that you are learning from a peer is one important strategy coaches use to build respect in a coaching relationship, but it isn't some artificial step they take to build a relationship. Peer Coaches insist that the insights they gain from collaborating with their peers help them improve their practice as teachers. Learning with and from their peers is a major part of what they love about coaching and why they continue to coach.

Personalized

If coaches want to personalize their coaching, they must understand that the needs of their learning partners must drive the collaboration between teacher and coach. This approach to shaping a coach's actions is what makes coaching so precise and valuable and leads to improved teaching and learning. It is differentiated instruction at its best. Coaches may understand the need to focus on others' professional needs, but it is a learned skill that takes time to develop. Coaches need a lot of experiences to avoid sentences that include "What I did…" or "In my classroom…"

> If coaches want to personalize their coaching, they must understand that the needs of their learning partners must drive the collaboration between teacher and coach.

One effective way to personalize a relationship is for the coach to determine what assistance the teacher feels he or she needs. Coaches then need to focus on listening, not talk too much, and make sure to ask how they can help. In addition to strong listening skills, some coaches, like Anna Walter, have observed another key to personalize the coaching relationship requires the emotional intelligence to "listen and acknowledge their ideas, their concerns and fears" (A. Walter, personal communication, September 28, 2011).

Many successful Peer Coaches use their first meeting with a new learning partner to personalize the relationship and make it clear to the peer that his or her needs will drive the work of the coaching partnership. Alessio Bernadelli says one of his goals for this initial meeting is to ensure the "coachee really needs to feel like they have a need that they can address by working with a coach" (A. Bernadelli, personal communication, July 11, 2011). The coach and collaborating teacher typically talk about the school's educational goals in this meeting and work to identify at least one learning activity the teacher feels she or he wants to improve to help reach these goals. The coach and teacher are defining a starting point for their relationship and making it clear that in this personalized relationship, the collaborating teacher's needs are paramount.

Manageable

Effective coaches have to work to balance the desire to improve learning with the need to keep the workload this effort imposes manageable. Coaches often note that they limit the scope of work their work with a partner because their colleague is already working at or near full capacity. You often hear teachers express this belief when they say, "I don't have the time for anything new." One Australian coach recognized this and tries to set reasonable goals and timeframes for action "so that my learning partner doesn't 'burn out'" (R. Grudic, personal communication, September 6, 2011). Strong coaches remind their learning partners that they might suggest different strategies to reach the teacher's goals, and coaches are quick to remind colleagues that they will be there to provide support. Effective coaches also take a measured approach to improving learning that is based on their assessment of their peer's capacity and readiness. This assessment may suggest to the coach the need to move ahead, but it could also suggest the need to go slow, start small, or even back off and wait. There are other reasons that a successful coach works to create a manageable workload.

Every coach needs to be very clear in his or her own mind that coaching is not a magical cure that will dramatically improve student learning overnight. Elmore's (2004) study of school reform led him to conclude that "Changing practice takes a long time and several cycles of trial and error" (p. 38). Peer Coaches' experiences demonstrate that improving instruction is a long-term, iterative process. It takes time. While a coach may be successful with improving some aspect of learning, like critical thinking skills, on the first effort, coaches also report it is more likely their peers may engage in several cycles of improving some aspect of their practice, including trying the new practice, getting feedback, and making additional revisions before they successfully make significant changes in their practice.

The Coaching Cycle (see Figure 1.1) represents a continuous improvement process that recognizes the stress already on teachers and emphasizes improvement over time. Teachers and coaches may choose to improve a learning activity by adopting one fairly clearly defined innovation, like grouping strategies, and assessing its impact. After setting goals, preparing, and implementing the learning activity, the coach and her learning partner turn to reflection. The information gathered in the reflection process after completing each learning activity gives teachers the opportunity to think about what worked, what didn't, and how they could apply what they learned from this experience in other similar learning activities. They may also focus on what they would do differently next time. The key here is that reflection doesn't mean

Figure 1.1   Coaching Cycle

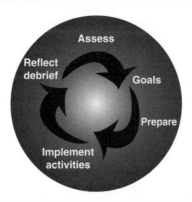

Source: Meyer et al. (2011e).

collaborating between a coach and teacher is "over and done." Reflection is part of an ongoing process of improvement. Reflection helps collaborating teacher and coach decide if they want to continue to work on the skill they focused on in this activity or move on to some other facet of improving learning. Even this brief description of the process of continuous improvement should suggest that dramatic improvements in classroom learning will take time. Many coaches report that they collaborate with the same teachers for years as they continue to work toward offering their students the kind of learning opportunities that will meet student needs.

Some prospective coaches have asked, when does this cycle of continuous improvement end? Judging when the relationship has successfully reached its conclusion is difficult. When I train coaches, I often use a synectic, a tool that asks participants to compare and contrast wildly incongruous items. One of these asks "How is Peer Coaching like or different from teaching rock climbing?" When I used this synectic at the Arizona Technology in Education Association's Shift-up coaching conference, one participant observed that "When the climber gets to the top of the rock the climbing student, and their instructor, know they have been successful, but…it isn't always so clear to the coach when they have success-fully reached the end of the coaching process" (L. Foltos, personal notes, November 5, 2011). Perhaps they won't reach the end. Student data, teachers' needs, and ongoing social and economic changes that drive educational change suggest that coaching will need to be part of an ongoing process of improvement.

Private

As I noted earlier, Peer Coaches play no role in evaluating teachers because that role would destroy the relationship of trust that is essential to successful coaching. This is not to say there is no communication about coaching between the coach and the school's administrators. Administrators often observe coaches and their peers collaborating, and effective coaches routinely brief the school's leaders on progress and challenges in their coaching work. Sustaining successful coaching pro-grams requires this kind of communication, but none of these efforts at communicating is designed to be part of the process of evaluating teachers.

Supported

As you read the roles coaches play and how Peer Coaches work to shape a friendly, personalized, manageable, and pri-vate relationship with their learning partners, you already see evidence of how a coach is building a supportive relationship. Effective coaches are careful to monitor how much support they are providing for their peer, because it is easy for a coach to cross the tipping point and take responsibility for the learn-ing away from the peer. Ken Kay and Valerie Greenhill (2012) noted that technology coaches in one school district were responsible for helping teachers use technology and over-all instructional improvement. "In reality, the coaches had become the 'go to' people directed by site leaders and teachers to attend to basic technology integration needs. The coaches had essentially become high-level gophers for teachers who had adopted a 'learned helplessness'" (p. 102). These coaches, with help from their administrators, rushed right past the tipping point; the coaches had assumed ownership of the learning happening in the coaching relationship.

Many experienced Peer Coaches, like Anna Walter, recognize that the coach needs to limit his or her responsibilities, or the teacher might "let the coach do everything; do all the work....If you want teachers to take ownership for learning, the coach can't be the expert" (A. Walter, personal communication, September 28, 2011). Like Socrates and Einstein, effective Peer Coaches believe that the primary responsibility for learning rests on the shoulders of those learning. Ensuring that the learner is taking responsibility for learning is a key strategy coaches use to help their peers develop the capacity to improve their teaching practices. In other words, the coach's role is to facilitate learning.

Instead of answering teachers' questions, coaches respond with questions designed to help their peers to formulate strategies designed to answer their questions. The coaches' role is to use inquiry to question current practices and encourage their learning partners to consider new practices and strategies. The coach may play an active role in helping the peer identify answers to the challenges they face, but ultimately the peer is making decisions and choosing a course of action. In this sense, Peer Coaching is very much like teaching rock climbing. As one coach noted, "At some point the person learning to climb has to be independent; so the instructor has to build the climber's capacity" (L. Foltos, personal notes, November 5, 2011). Coaching is much the same. Teachers won't grow professionally; they won't have the capacity to improve their craft if their coach tells them what do to. Successful coaches build capacity, not dependence.

> Successful coaches build capacity, not dependence.

To avoid crossing the tipping point and taking ownership of the learning, successful coaches discuss and develop the roles they will play with their peers and school leadership. These same discussions should help the coach's learning partner to define the roles and responsibilities they will assume as they work with a coach. By defining these roles and responsibilities, the coach and their learning partners are also are working to create individual and collective accountability for learning in a way that assigns the primary responsibility for learning to the collaborating teacher. This basic set of roles and responsibilities is critical to building an effective supportive coaching relationship. Without agreement on roles and responsibilities, the coach and their peers may find that coaching can potentially founder or fail.

Coaches need to understand that their success depends on more than establishing a coaching relationship that is friendly, personalized, manageable, private, and supported. Ultimately, their success as coaches will depend on their ability to create relationships based on trust and respect.

RELATIONSHIPS, RESPECT, AND TRUST

Linda King is a teacher-librarian from Yakima who has been a Peer Coach for several years. When asked how she measured her success as a coach, it took her mere seconds to distill what she had learned from her experiences. "You know you're successful as a coach when teachers are willing to share what they know and willing to share what they do not know" (L. King, personal communication, October 2010). No one who has heard or read her remarkably concise thoughts has ever missed King's point. The coach and his or her learning partners are trying to improve learning, but the coach may also be moving the teacher out of his or her comfort zone, encouraging the teacher to take risks and maybe to fail publically. Developing a relationship based on respect and trust between coach and learning partner is nonnegotiable for successful coaching.

> Developing a relationship based on respect and trust between coach and learning partner is nonnegotiable for successful coaching.

If you review the Building Blocks of Trust (see Figure 1.2), you will see that what coaches say or do as they work to build a personalized, friendly, manageable, supportive relationship goes a long way toward building respect and trust. We have talked about what coaches might say to build trust, and it is important to note that the coach's actions are equally important. Many teachers new to working with a coach feel like they are imposing when they ask a coach for assistance. They know how busy the coach's day is and imagine that they are taking valuable time from him or her. Imagine their reaction if the coach's door is always closed or the coach is consistently too busy to talk in the hallway or teachers' lounge. Actions count.

The Building Blocks of Trust also help us understand that the roles a coach plays in collaborating with a learning partner are important; how the coach carries out those roles is critical. Experienced Peer Coaches realize that they can and must do more to create a relationship based on trust and respect. As we explore these additional steps coaches take to create a trusting, respectful relationship, let's keep in mind

Figure 1.2   Building Blocks of Trust

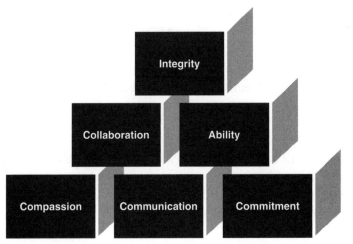

Source: Meyer et al. (2011w).

the idea that what coaches do is important; how they do it shapes their success or failure.

Expert vs. Trust

Many coaches who are just getting started ultimately have a very simple question: When can they tell collaborating teachers what to do? They are asking when the coach should play the role of expert. We briefly explored this issue earlier, so it shouldn't be surprising that every coach asks this same question at some point. While coaches don't want to be tagged with the label "expert," they do sense a dilemma. Many veteran coaches recognize there may be many reasons to take on the role of expert. They understand that their success requires that they have a proven track record of successful innovation working in their environment. They know that peers want a coach who could provide useful, relevant examples. Peer Coaches understand that coach training helped them develop a variety of new skills and expertise and that their peers may expect them to be the expert with the answers. So when is the time right for a coach to assume the role of expert and tell peers what to do and how to do it? Clearly, this is a serious dilemma. The way coaches respond to this dilemma seems simple, but it is fairly nuanced.

Let's start to answer that question by asking what their peers really expect from their coach. Over the years, I have asked teachers who collaborate with coaches to define some of the attributes of a successful coach. Some of these attributes include:

- Is able to build trust with peers
- Builds on what a teacher needs
- Communicates well and listens to teachers
- Is flexible
- Provides a safe, risk-taking environment and is non-threatening, nonjudgmental, and accepting
- Is recognized by staff as a strong/outstanding teacher (Meyer et al., 2011c)

Even a brief reading of these attributes makes it clear teachers want a coach to be a peer, not an expert. This is consistent with what collaborating teachers say in their assessments of coaching. Not one of them has written, "Thank goodness I have someone coming into my classroom to tell me what to do." They clearly don't want an expert telling them what to think or do, but they do want a knowledgeable, skilled coach. The word *expert* has a negative connotation for these teachers.

I often walk away from conversations with Peer Coaches believing that the need to be seen as a peer must be a part of a successful coach's DNA. Experienced coaches seem to understand instinctively that if coaches position themselves as experts, their colleagues may feel inferior. Coaches have told me that few teachers will want to work with coaches who have put themselves on a pedestal. By contrast, if they build a relationship in which the collaborating teacher sees the coach as a peer, the coach would have created the sense of equality. Alessio Bernadelli, a Welsh Peer Coach, insists this sense of equality is critical to "promote honest dialogue about what the peer wants to develop" (A. Bernadelli, personal communication, July 11, 2011). Being seen as a peer is an essential first step to a coach's success. But it is only a first step. A coach must develop a relationship as a true peer before taking on the role of expert in the coaching relationship. With time and experience, coaches understand that their colleagues will come to see them as true peers, but peers that have unique and valuable expertise.

The real irony here is that expertise is essential for Peer Coaches who want to avoid taking on the role of expert. As we will see in subsequent chapters, coaches who know how to use communication, lesson-design, and technology-integration skills do not take responsibility for learning away from a peer the way an expert would. Instead of telling their peers what to do and how to do it, they use these their expertise and skills to help their peers develop their capacity to improve teaching and learning.

These successful coaches have several important messages about building trust.

- It is important for coaches to recognize that they are peers, not experts.

- Coaches don't see egalitarianism as a roadblock to their success but as a key to open the door to their success.

> Coaches don't see egalitarianism as a roadblock to their success but as a key to open the door to their success.

- One of those building blocks of trust (see Figure 1.2) is collaboration. It is hard to argue that playing the role of expert and telling peers what to think and do is consistent with the idea of collaboration.

- If a coach wants to be effective at collaboration, coaching expertise is far more important than being an expert.

How Coaches Carry Out Roles

Coaches who want to create relationships based on respect and trust must understand that the roles they play as a coach are important, but how they coach is critical. In conversations about when it is appropriate for a coach to tell a peer what to think and do, experienced Peer Coaches offer us some insights into how effective coaches practice their craft.

Since effective coaches recognize that telling peers what to think and do breaks the relationship of trust the coaches are trying to build, they are very selective about when they choose to tell peers what they think. Paul Shanahan warned that before he advocates any idea, he weighs where he is in the relationship with a collaborating teacher. "Early on it is questioning, questioning, questioning. In year two or year three of a relationship, and you have something to give, they may want it. So you tell them what you think" (P. Shanahan, personal communication, September 6, 2011). Like Shanahan, many coaches take on the role of expert only when invited by a colleague and even then ask "Would you like me to share my ideas?" before offering an opinion.

So if they are not telling peers what to think or do, what produces improvements in teaching and learning?

Effective coaches try to emphasize inquiry over advocacy in their coaching work. In other words, they rely on questioning strategies rather than advocating for any particular solution to the issues facing their peers. An Australian Peer Coach offered a view shared by many coaches when he said that the balance needs to be tipped to the probing questions and coaching. He rarely relied on sharing his answer, and did so "only when the trust and respect is there" (L. Foltos, personal notes, August 2011). By emphasizing inquiry over advocacy, these coaches are taking another step to build a relationship based on trust and respect. They are also helping their learning partners build their capacity to improve teaching and learning instead of creating a dependence on the coach.

Coaching can't succeed without a trusting, respectful relationship between the coach and the collaborating teacher. Fortunately, trust isn't a precondition for a coach to begin collaborating with a teacher. It is equally lucky that coaches do not need to have an innate Zen-like understanding of how to build trust. Coach training can help a coach develop an understanding

> Coaching can't succeed without a trusting, respectful relationship between the coach and the collaborating teacher.

of how to establish trust and respect. Collaborating with other experienced coaches can help a coach develop an even keener appreciation of how his or her behavior can build the kind of relationship essential to successful coaching. Even the most successful coaches realize that coaching experience is essential to help them develop trust and respect over time. As a coach who was in his first year of coaching noted, "I have learned to step back and to try not to impose my ideas. I have learned to become a better listener." A second coach reported to program evaluators, "I realize the importance of being a good listener and finding out what someone else's needs are. I have also learned that I can't force someone to do something" (Liston, Peterson, & Ragan, 2008, p. 68).

Peer Coaching is a powerful learning methodology only when coaches are successful in creating trusting relationships with peers. This relationship forms a safety net that is essential to encourage the coach's learning partner to take the risks necessary to improve instruction. It helps teachers face their fear factor. We will explore how coaches move beyond this initial stage in their relationship with their peers in the following chapters.

Summary

Einstein insisted that his role in the learning process was to create the conditions for learning. Effective coaches do the same thing by:

- Collaborating with a colleague to improve teaching and learning to prepare students with the skills and competencies they need for college or careers.
- Recognizing that many schools don't have a culture that supports collaboration and risk taking.
- Being a peer who takes the lead in creating a relationship based on trust and respect.
  - Coaches are most successful when these relationships are friendly, personalized, manageable, private, and supported.
  - Successful coaches are careful to ensure what they say and how they act is consistent with their goal of building trust.
- Building trust by eschewing the roles an expert might typically take. Instead, they:
  - Work with peers to define the roles and responsibilities each will have in the coaching relationship.
  - Use their coaching expertise to provide the support teachers might need and use inquiry and other strategies to maintain their learning partners' ownership of their learning.

2

Why Peer Coaching?

It is time for our education workforce to engage in learning the way other professionals do—continually, collaboratively, and on the job—to address common problems and crucial challenges where they work.

—Former North Carolina Governor James Hunt

After reading the last chapter, you might have the impression that economic and social changes require educational change and that coaching is the answer to produce change. The conclusion might be premature. It certainly isn't one that educational and political leaders have reached. Virtually all educational leaders today believe schools need to change, and they all seem to have an agenda for change. Unfortunately, *change* is a terribly imprecise word. According to Merriam Webster, *change* can mean "to make different." There is nothing in the definition of the word that suggests improvement. That hasn't stopped educators from focusing on changing education. While there is nothing close to an agreement on an agenda for change, there are many common prescriptions for how to make education different. For many policy and educational leaders, these prescriptions for change include reducing class sizes, making the school day or school year longer, altering schools' governance structures by creating more charter schools, or offering teachers merit pay. While there are plenty of advocates for each of these ideas, over the last decade, the loudest and most persistent discussion about what will change education has focused on the need for more accountability for schools and educators.

We have all heard supporters of more accountability argue that change happens through assessment. To anyone who grew up on or near a farm, it is clear that ranchers learned long ago that they need to do more than weigh the cattle daily to fatten them up. Perhaps there is a lesson here for education. Are any of these prescriptions for "change" likely to produce the profound transformation of learning that social and economic changes dictate? Will these prescriptions help students develop 21st-century skills? In his work on the "drivers" of systemic reform, Michael Fullan (2011a) argues that there is a clear lack of compelling evidence that any of these prescriptions will produce the kind of results we as a nation want for our schools. What's missing from any of these prescriptions for change is an emphasis on two important elements in the equation for improving student performance.

> We have all heard supporters of more accountability argue that change happens through assessment. To anyone who grew up on or near a farm, it is clear that ranchers learned long ago that they need to do more than weigh the cattle daily to fatten them up.

Barber and Mourshed's (2007) study of the world's top-performing schools systems helps us refocus on what is likely to improve student learning. They found that these school systems improved student learning on the PISA test by acting on the assumption that "the only way to improve outcomes is to improve instruction" (p. 26). This same research found that this corollary was obvious to the same school systems; they all emphasize improving the quality of their teachers.

I have shared Barber and Mourshed's findings with thousands of educators around the world and have yet to find one who disagrees with these conclusions. Educators know that improving student learning is inextricably tied to what happens in the classroom between the teacher and the student. These educators understand that they must improve their practice to improve student outcomes. If we listen, teachers say they need assistance defining what effective teaching and learning looks like and how to implement this vision for learning. What conclusion can we draw from this research and the ideas held by many teachers?

- Helping teachers to develop critical thinking, creativity, communication, and collaboration skills is the first step toward offering students learning activities designed to develop these same skills.

  > Helping teachers to develop critical thinking, creativity, communication, and collaboration skills is the first step toward offering students learning activities designed to develop these same skills.

- Professional learning must develop each educator's capacity to improve teaching and learning.
- The key to improving student learning is the professional learning schools and school systems provide for their teachers.

PROFESSIONAL DEVELOPMENT: WISHFUL THINKING

Educational, political, and business leaders understand that traditional instruction alone won't help meet students' needs, but there is far less understanding that the way we prepare teachers hinders efforts to improve student learning. In fact, what school systems do to prepare teachers seems to be shaped by wishful thinking. Stephen Fink, the executive director of the University of Washington's Center for

Educational Leadership, insists that American educational and political leaders act as if we can help the vast majority of teachers to get better "with a limited amount of training. Nothing could be further from the truth" (Shaw, 2011). In their work, *Professional Learning in the Learning Profession*, Linda Darling-Hammond and colleagues (2009) offered a wealth of evidence to support Fink's conclusions. They found that teachers need about 50 hours of professional development to improve in a specific area. Unfortunately, their research revealed that most American teachers participate in short-term conferences or workshops instead of intensive professional learning. The quantity of professional learning teachers participate in is only half of the problem.

Darling-Hammond and colleagues (2009) also examined the qualities of that professional development the teachers participated in. They concluded that collaboration among teachers promoted school change and that when teachers across the school collaborated, all the students in the school benefited. They found that educators in the United States are one of the few groups of professionals that have not routinely relied on professional collaboration to improve their practice.

So what conclusions can we draw about the kind of professional development offered to most teachers in the United States? The equation is as simple as quality plus quantity, so this problem is easy to solve. Darling-Hammond and colleagues (2009) drew a simple, scathing conclusion that the training teachers "receive is episodic, myopic, and often meaningless" (p. 2). While much of the evidence shaping the findings in *Professional Learning in the Learning Profession* is new, many of the conclusions are far from

> The training teachers...receive is episodic, myopic, and often meaningless.
>
> —Darling-Hammond et al. (2009, p. 2)

original. Over the last 25 years, Bruce Showers and Beverly Joyce have assessed the impact of training on teachers' classroom practice. They reported (see Table 2.1) that most professional development focused on learning theory and how to

Table 2.1   Impact of Professional Development

Type of Training	Classroom Application
Theory +	5–10%
Practice +	10–15%
Coaching, study teams, peer visits	80–90%

Source: Meyer et al (2011z).

put theory into practice. Teachers use this kind of learning in their classroom practice no more than 15% of the time (Joyce & Showers, 1994, 2002; Showers, Murphy, & Joyce, 1996).

PROFESSIONAL LEARNING THAT WORKS

It is quite clear that educational institutions are experienced at offering professional development that doesn't affect classroom practice; what do we know about professional learning that will help teachers improve their practice? If we ask both educators and researchers, it turns out we know quite a lot.

Improving Practice Can Only Be Done by Teachers, Not to Teachers

Educational leaders have long acted on the belief that they can introduce their vision for change and teachers will buy into and implement that vision. We all are familiar with this model; educational leaders, who are often far removed from classrooms, devise or adopt a solution and mandate its implementation. Innovation arrives at the classroom door in the form of new textbook adoptions, new curriculum, or new approaches to pedagogy. Each teacher is expected to take the innovation and implement it as prescribed in his or her classroom. Some literacy programs assign coaches to help teachers adopt the innovation and monitor the teachers to ensure fidelity to the program. In its most extreme form, educators are more like cogs in an assembly line, not partners in efforts to foster innovation. Sometimes we even hear this sort of reform being described as an effort to make the curriculum "teacher proof."

No matter how the model is implemented, research shows that externally imposed reforms have been singularly unimpressive. Richard Elmore's (2004) study of 100 years of educational reform efforts in the United States led him to conclude that only about 25% of teachers bought into these reforms. Researchers who examined the impact of externally imposed reform in several European countries and Australia echoed Elmore's findings (Mulford, 2003; van den Berg, Vandenberghe, & Sleegers, 1999). No matter where it is tried, this approach has failed because it impinges on teachers' professionalism. It makes educators technicians rather than encouraging them to be creative professionals (Hargreaves, 2003; van den Berg et al., 1999; Wurtzel, 2007).

In recent years, a number of educators have offered another avenue to innovation; their approach embraces Wurtzel's (2007) contention that teachers hold the power to improve. This group of researchers and practitioners believes that the only way forward is to empower teachers to embrace the responsibility for improving teaching and learning and for school systems to support teachers' efforts (Fullan, 2011a; Fullan & Hargraves, 2012). This research, and my experiences over more than two decades, suggests that urging teachers to change without empowering them will continue to fail to improve student learning.

> This research, and my experiences over more than two decades, suggests that urging teachers to change without empowering them will continue to fail to improve student learning.

One element of empowering teachers could be to ask them what kind of professional learning might help them improve. The results of this sort of inquiry are enlightening. In the past decade, members of the Peer Coaching team have asked thousands of educators to think of a professional-development experience that changed their practice as educators and to define what made the experience so effective. In other words, the educators are defining the characteristics of effective professional learning. In August 2010, one group of educators from across New South Wales, Australia, participated in this discussion. Their traits of effective professional development included:

- Just in time
- Backed up by compelling research or evidence
- Applying the learning to practice, not just doing the theory!
- Collaborative
- Links to quality teaching
- The professional learning was directly related to a classroom problem
- Had opportunity to apply what I learned in a lesson, then reflect and discuss
- Professional learning was directly aligned to student engagement and achievement!
- Targeted in on what it was that I needed development in and met that need with specific follow up. (L. Foltos, personal notes, July 25, 2011)

To summarize, they felt professional learning needed to be driven by student and teacher needs, immediately relevant to their classroom problems, reflective, ongoing, and collaborative. The qualities they defined are identical to those of educators from around the world who have engaged in this same activity. It should not be too surprising that these educators' insights are supported by a growing body of research on effective professional development.

CHARACTERISTICS OF EFFECTIVE PROFESSIONAL DEVELOPMENT

Highly Collaborative

For more than 20 years, Joyce and Showers have observed that professional development that included opportunities for collaboration and reflection improved the impact of training in rather startling ways. As Table 2.1 demonstrates, teachers who participate in professional learning methodologies that promote collaboration and offer them opportunities for reflection apply what they learn nearly 90% of the time (Joyce & Showers, 1994, 2002; Showers et al., 1996). There is a wealth of research to support the value of collaboration among educators.

Barber and Mourshed's (2007) study of the world's top-performing school systems found that they enable teachers to work together and learn from one another while planning lessons jointly and observing each other teaching (p. 26). Enabling teachers to work together was so important that the school system provided teachers with the time and other resources necessary for regular, routine collaboration, and the support of a peer coach. Darling-Hammond's group (2009) found that "when all teachers in a school learn together, all students in the school benefit" (p. 5). Michael Fullan has argued for more than a decade that collaboration among educators is essential to systemwide improvements in learning (Fullan, 2001, 2008, 2011b).

> *When all teachers in a school learn together, all students in the school benefit.*
> —Darling-Hammond et al. (2009, p. 5)

Intensive and Ongoing

Professional development needs to be intensive and ongoing, because the process of improving teaching and learning is not often smooth or instantly successful. In the first chapter, we observed that coaches work with colleagues by modeling or coteaching a lesson or observing a peer. In both cases, the coach and learning partner reflect afterward to discuss what worked and what could be improved and

> Adapting and adopting innovative practices can be a bumpy process that includes taking risks, making mistakes, and learning from them. It is a long-term process of continuous improvement!

to celebrate even small successes. Adapting and adopting innovative practices can be a bumpy process that includes taking risks, making mistakes, and learning from them. It is a long-term process of continuous improvement!

There is another reason educators need and want intensive, long-term professional development: They have seen too much of the opposite. Earlier we noted the wide number of prescriptions for change that schools might be asked to adopt. This list of prescriptions doesn't include changes that result from adoptions of new curriculum materials, new assessment or teaching strategies, or new professional-development methodologies. Teachers may be buried by all of the prescriptions for change they are asked to adopt. Michael Fullan (2001) noted that some schools might have 11 significant initiatives underway simultaneously, so many that they frustrate and anger teachers. Fullan's observations aren't unique. If you're an educator, you have probably known teachers who listen to presentations meant to motivate them about the next innovation they are being asked to adopt. And as they walk into their classrooms and close the door, the last words you heard from these teachers are, "And this too shall pass." Elmore (2004) is so convinced that improving learning takes time and focus that he insists one major design principle for school districts is "to organize everyone's actions, at all levels of the system, around an instructional focus that is stable over time" (p. 80).

On the Job, Connected to Classroom Practice

We have noted that teachers believe there has to be an immediate link between professional development and what they need to know to meet the needs of students in their classrooms. Research aligns perfectly with the beliefs of these teachers. The subject professional development focuses on is critical, and so is the location at which that learning occurs. The coaches we talked about in the first chapter worked with peers to coplan learning activities, model or team-teach effective learning, and observe their colleagues and engage in reflective discussions afterward. This kind of professional learning isn't going to happen at professional-development events that are held outside their school building. Barber and Mourshed (2007) found that teachers in the world's top-performing school systems collaborate in the most relevant and effective location: while working in their classrooms.

Educators and researchers have learned a lot about the characteristics of effective professional learning. But what have educators done with this knowledge? Richard Elmore (2004) has observed that schools may know what kind of professional development is effective, but they haven't acted on that knowledge. You don't have to visit many schools before you realize that many continue to encourage teachers to participate in workshops and offer few opportunities for meaningful collaboration. Other schools are finding ways to put knowledge into action.

PEER COACHING AND EFFECTIVE PROFESSIONAL LEARNING

> The world's best-performing school systems, Barber and Mourshed (2007) found, all recognize "if you want good teachers, you need to have good teachers train them, and this requires focused one-on-one coaching in the classroom" (p. 28).

The world's best-performing school systems, Barber and Mourshed (2007) found, all recognize "if you want good teachers, you need to have good teachers train them, and this requires focused one-on-one coaching in the classroom" (p. 28). In these highly successful school systems, coaches go into classrooms to provide feedback, model better instruction, and help teachers reflect on their practice. Classroom teachers I have worked with certainly agree with this conclusion.

Microsoft chose nearly 70 teachers to participate in a Worldwide Innovative Teachers Forum in 2007. They were chosen because they were offering students the kind of innovative learning experiences that would help their students develop the necessary skills in core content areas and 21st-century skills. Yet none of these educators reported that their innovative practices had been adopted by other educators, not even by colleagues in their schools. Their work was both remarkably innovative and remarkably insular. I was lucky enough to facilitate their conversation about what would be required to spread their innovative practices widely among other teachers. These innovative educators were unanimous on one point: Teachers are likely to need encouragement, support, and assistance to adapt and adopt innovative learning activities. They need a peer to:

- Help them understand why they should adopt an innovative practice
- Help weigh the costs of adopting the innovation as they compare the benefits for students to the time and effort required to implement an innovative learning activity
- Provide just enough just-in-time support, training, and resources
- Coplan learning activities
- Model learning activities or team-teach with them
- Reflect and debrief with after they try an innovative activity (L. Foltos, personal notes, November 2007)

These innovative teachers concluded that if schools want wide-scale adoption of innovative practices, teachers need a mentor or coach at each step in the process of adaptation and adoption.

> If schools want wide-scale adoption of innovative practices, teachers need a mentor or coach at each step in the process of adaptation and adoption.

Even this cursory review of their conclusions reveals that these innovative educators are telling us that the support their peers need to adopt innovative practices must be highly collaborative, intensive, and ongoing, implemented on the job, and focused on student needs. Their ideas about the kind of support teachers need to adopt innovative practices align perfectly with what research tells us about effective professional learning. These innovative educators urged the use of coaches or mentors to assist educators working to adopt innovative teaching practices because coaching is exactly the kind of methodology that can turn these ideas about effective professional learning into practice. They are right on this key point. In Chapter 1, we described coaching as an ongoing process of continuous improvement of teaching and learning that relied on coaches who coplan learning activities, model and team-teach, and observe their peers and reflect afterward. This type of coaching is the embodiment of the research on effective professional learning.

PEER COACHES' EFFECTIVENESS

One indication that Peer Coaching is effective is how easily it goes viral. Coaches call this the ripple effect. Let's look at an example of the ripple effect.

Riding the Wave of the Ripple Effect

Pat Matsuzawa, one of the very first participants in Peer Coaching, was the teacher librarian for a large high school. Her initial learning partner was an American history teacher, and they decided to collaborate to improve a lesson on the presidency. The teacher had been asking his students to choose an American president, research that president, and submit a short written report. He was concerned that reports tended to emphasize facts. After revising the activity with his coach, the history teacher asked teams of students to assume the role of a committee to re-elect a president. Each team of students chose its president, researched the president's first term in office, and wrote a campaign plan to re-elect the president based on his accomplishment. To demonstrate learning and get feedback, each re-election committee would present its re-election plan to the class. Clearly this was more than a simple factual written report.

Still, the history teacher wasn't convinced about the new learning activity. He taught several American history classes but decided to try this improved activity in only one. Before his students had completed this activity, their critical thinking, communication, and collaboration convinced the history teacher to use the revised activity in every class in the future. He began to talk to Pat about other lessons they might collaborate on to make them more effective.

Soon there was a ripple effect that quickly spread beyond Pat and her colleague. Other history teachers approached Pat saying they had heard about the presidents lesson and asked how they could be "one of the chosen ones" and work with Pat. They were pulled to coaching, and that pull produced a ripple that expanded the scope of coaching. Pat began working with other history teachers, but the ripple didn't stop there. Within a year, biology and English teachers were asking Pat to collaborate with them. Pat did, and at the same time, the school recognized the value of coaching by having several other educators trained as coaches (P. Matsuzawa, personal communication, March 3, 2004).

Successful Peer Coaches all seem to have a story about how the ripple effect provides proof that their work as a coach is making an impact on their colleagues' teaching and learning. There is additional evidence of the impact of Peer Coaching that comes from evaluations of Peer Coaching in two states.

Washington State: Enhanced Peer Coaching

Throughout this chapter we have focused on the importance of collaboration as a key to improving teaching and learning. Both coaches and their collaborating teachers told evaluators of a Peer Coaching program in Washington State that coaching provided structure and a nonthreatening environment for teachers to collaborate that improves instruction (Liston, Peterson, & Ragan, 2008).

> [My coach] is my safety net and it allowed me to experiment more than I would have otherwise.
> —Liston & Ragan (2009, p. 77)

Both collaborating teachers and their principals reported that Peer Coaches gave teachers the confidence to stretch and to take risks and be innovative. One collaborating teacher explained the role the coach played when she said, "[My coach] is my safety net and it allowed me to experiment more than I would have otherwise" (Liston & Ragan, 2009, p. 77).

Collaborating with a Peer Coach also helped teachers improve teaching and learning. Program evaluators used assessment tools to measure changes in classroom practice over time. These evaluators concluded that collaboration with a Peer Coach increased the teachers' confidence and willingness to use technology in the classroom in ways that engage students in learning. In 2009, for example, 25% of the collaborating teachers reported that after 1 year of working with a coach, they had moved from using technology primarily as a productivity tool to using it to support active engaged student learning (Liston & Ragan, 2009). After interviewing Peer Coaches, collaborating teachers, and principals, program evaluators concluded that Peer Coaches helped collaborating teachers reshape student learning by offering more challenging, engaging learning activities to help them develop critical thinking and problem-solving skills. As a collaborating teacher told program evaluators, "The students' learning has been affected positively with the work I have done with my peer coach. Learning has become more engaged and fun for the students. The instruction has become more student-centered and less teacher-centered" (Liston & Ragan, 2009, p. 81). These kinds of changes are not unique to those who participate in Peer Coaching in Washington.

Wisconsin's Peer Coaching Collaborative

Mary Lou Ley, the facilitator who leads Wisconsin's Peer Coaching Collaborative, shared some of what she had learned as a result of their experiences with Peer Coaching in a webinar. Ley explained the ways coaches use probing questions to move beyond the friendly, supportive relationship between teacher and coach and encourage collaborating teachers to take risks to improve teaching and learning. Her evaluation of Peer Coaching found that 71% of participants in Wisconsin felt coaching made a significant impact on their ability to use technology to promote critical thinking and problem solving, engage students in learning, and improve academic curricula (Ley, 2011).

> Seventy-one percent of participants in Wisconsin felt coaching made a significant impact on their ability to use technology to promote critical thinking and problem solving, engage students in learning, and improve academic curricula (Ley, 2011).

Ley and her team collected examples of learning activities from participants at the start of their coaching experience and again after educators had considerable experience collaborating with their Peer Coaches. The evaluation team looked at indicators of quality like cognitive challenge, inquiry, collaboration, real-world connections, and the level of technology use to assess these learning activities. Their assessment showed that more than 70% of the learning activities collected prior to significant coaching experience scored at a low level using these quality indicators. After participating in coaching throughout the assessment year, these same educators submitted examples of learning activities that reflected their coaching experiences. When judged by the same set of quality indicators, evaluators found that nearly 60% of the educators' learning activities were "High Quality" (Ley, 2011).

Summary

The need to improve education to better prepares students with 21st-century skills like critical thinking, communication, collaboration, and creativity is clear. Schools and school systems have by and large not adapted to meet this challenge.

(Continued)

(Continued)

- Their efforts have focused on a change agenda that has little to do with improving student learning and put far too little emphasis on improving instruction to increase student achievement.
- American educational and political leaders act as if we can help the vast majority of teachers to improve teaching and learning with only a minimal investment in professional development. The limited amount spent often focuses on ineffectual training.
- Both highly innovative educators and educational researchers agree. Effective professional learning is:

  o Highly collaborative
  o Intensive and ongoing
  o On the job
  o Focused on classroom needs
  o Aligned with schools' educational goals

- Coaching puts into practice what we know about effective professional learning. Peer Coaches are the catalysts that can help other educators implement innovative learning activities and help their students develop the skills they need for college and careers.

3

Preparing Coaches

The emerging science of learning underscores the importance of rethinking what is taught, how it is taught, and how learning is assessed.

—Bransford, Brown, & Cocking (2000)

As we noted in the first chapter, many educators have helped other teachers to improve instruction. Teachers shouldn't expect that occasional collaboration with a peer has prepared them to take on the roles a coach plays. Educational leaders also need to recognize that there is a vast difference between what some teachers are already doing and effective coaching. Unfortunately, many American school administrators have identified educators with strong content skills and, without providing them with any formal preparation, given them a new role: coach.

What these educational leaders are actually doing is similar to what happens in many movies set in the Old West.

Early in these westerns, small towns lose their sheriffs in some violent incident that leaves the town helpless in the face of evil. The town's leaders invariably respond by pinning the sheriff's badge on the first available candidate. On incredibly rare occasions, the new sheriff is Clint Eastwood. More often, the new sheriff is an unknown character actor whose primary qualification is that he happened to be available. We have all seen enough of these movies to know his fate is about as promising as his acting career.

Like Hollywood's sheriffs, coaches who have the recognition that comes with their title but little or no training to prepare them to fulfill their role are likely to be about as successful. Richards (2003) argues school-based professional developers fail because they lack experience, have poor communications skills, and have limited preparation. Unprepared coaches affect others as well. Gawande (2011), in a *New Yorker* article, argues, "bad coaching can make people worse." Schools that fail to provide careful training are demeaning the profession and the coach and the teachers they collaborate with. There is a large and growing variety of coaches in schools today. A partial list includes literacy coaches, math coaches, data coaches, instructional coaches, curriculum coaches, and peer coaches. Whatever they are called, the educators who play these roles may not need badges, but they clearly need careful training and experience to be successful.

> *Bad coaching can make people worse.*
> —Gawande (2011)

WHO COACHES AND WHY?

Peer Coaches are teacher leaders who assist their peers to engage students in pedagogically powerful learning activities that will prepare them for college and careers. In short, they are working to help teachers become more innovative and effective. So who coaches? Peer Coaches are typically teachers and teacher librarians. In some cases, they are school administrators. Most of the Peer Coaches we have worked with span the K–12 spectrum, but a small number are university professors. Coaches come from every content area. There is one common denominator that ties all of them together: Peer Coaches have classroom experience, often in the school where they will be coaching. Without classroom experience, they will not have the credibility they need to be trusted by their peers.

> There is one common denominator that ties all of them together: Peer Coaches have classroom experience, often in the school where they will be coaching. Without classroom experience, they will not have the credibility they need to be trusted by their peers.

If the coach has previously taught in the school where he or she is coaching, that person has successfully used innovative learning activities with the same group of students his or her peers teach. This kind of experience is invaluable. I would be rich if I got a dollar for every time I heard a teacher say that an innovative learning activity may work for teachers in another school, but that it won't work with "our" students. Coaches who have successfully used innovative learning activities have the perfect response for their peers who question whether this innovation will work with their students: "It does, and I can model it for you."

Classroom experience in the same school where they coach offers coaches several other advantages. Each school is a unique community whose participants (students, teachers, staff, administrators, parents, and business partners) shape its culture, making its routines and processes unlike any other school. Peer Coaches who coach in their home schools will have a deeper appreciation of the schools' environments. As they begin their work as coaches, they already have an understanding of the school's curriculum, its assessment procedures, its students, its culture, and its staff. This kind of understanding is essential to successful coaching. If the process of choosing coaches is effective, it is likely that colleagues already recognize the coaches as strong or outstanding teachers, which makes it more likely that their peers will want to work with them.

But this isn't to say that coaches *must* come from the school where they coach. Coaches who come from outside the school can gain all of the key information and insights and build relationships. But it will take time. Several years ago, I was speaking to a highly successful coach who worked in his home school for half the day and was just beginning to coach in a new school the other half of the day. By mid-year, he offered a long list of coaching accomplishments in his home school, but he was strangely quiet on his work in the new school. When I asked about his successes in the new school, he noted he was still building relationships and trust and learning about the school (P. Shanahan, personal communication, January 6, 2004). If you want coaching to have an immediate impact, insiders have a clear advantage since they know the environment and their peers know and respect them.

Coaching is a lot of work. Hard work. Coaches who are assigned to coach full time or half the school day are obviously compensated for their work. The vast majority of the Peer Coaches are full-time classroom teachers or teacher librarians. Their schools may provide time and other resources to coach, but it is rare to hear of schools that provide a stipend or any other form of financial compensation. Shrinking educational budgets seem to be pushing some schools to adopt coaching only if there are no additional staffing costs. So why would a full-time teacher want to add to his or her workload by coaching?

Conversations with Peer Coaches reveal that most are drawn to coaching by their belief that collaboration with peers is the key to improving student learning, and they feel Peer Coaching offers the right conditions for successful collaboration. There are some teachers who became coaches because they hoped to move from the classroom into full-time roles providing professional development or to become principals. They see coaching as a great professional stepping stone. Many more Peer Coaches have more altruistic reasons for coaching. Anna Walter said she became a Peer Coach because "there were really good people in the school and I had a personal desire to support others and work with them...to see the effects of really good teaching on kids" (A. Walter, personal communication, September 28, 2011). Like Walter, many Peer Coaches have told me that they coach because they like learning with and from their peers. Time after time, I have heard Peer Coaches express the belief that their coaching experiences improve their teaching practice and they are empowering peers to improve student learning. Many Peer Coaches, like Shona Brooks, report they coach others because they get "satisfaction from helping other teachers develop skills and gain confidence" (S. Brooks, personal communication, August 3, 2011). This sense that Peer Coaches empower peers to improve is an incredibly strong motivation for both beginning coaches and those who have been practicing their craft for years.

FROM TEACHER LEADER TO COACH: WHAT DO PEER COACHES NEED TO KNOW?

Most educators begin Peer Coach training with some sense of the gaps between what they know and the skills they believe they need to help other educators improve instruction. The first activities in Peer Coach training ask prospective Peer Coaches to identify their coaching goals, roles, and responsibilities and to start to define a coaching plan. At this point,

> Prospective Peer Coaches often feel unprepared for the challenge and want to know more about how coach training will prepare them to assume their coaching roles.

they tend to become nervous. Many wonder what they have gotten themselves into. Most know they will be teaching full time and will have scant time to devote to coaching. Even if they will be released from teaching full or part time, the coach's task looks huge since one of the key goals of every coach is to help teachers improve learning. Prospective Peer

Coaches often feel unprepared for the challenge and want to know more about how coach training will prepare them to assume their coaching roles.

Part of the training Peer Coaches experience asks them to begin to define the skills and competencies they think they will need to be successful coaches. To prompt their thinking and discussions, these teacher leaders review and discuss this scenario:

> *You are meeting with a colleague you are coaching later today. He has been offering a traditional research assignment to students for several years. In this assignment, students are asked to do research on a given topic, for example, the presidency of Thomas Jefferson, and complete a five-page paper. During the meeting, the teacher wants to discuss the activity with you and come up with some ideas on how to improve this assignment. How can the coach help this teacher?* (Meyer et al., 2011s)

After reading this scenario, many coaches are thinking, "This teacher genuinely wants help. How do I begin to provide assistance?" Coach training asks three questions about how to assist this teacher and how to define what a coach needs to know and be able to do to help a peer.

1. What skills and competencies do our students need to be successful in college and their careers?

2. What are the characteristics of learning activities that will help students develop these skills?

3. What professional learning is going to best prepare teachers to meet their students' needs? (Meyer et al., 2011s)

While the activity asks coaches to think about all three of these questions, the facilitator leading the discussion follows Steven Covey's axiom, "begin with the end in mind" (Covey, 2004). All of a coach's work derives from or is driven by students' needs. Coming to an agreement on what skills and competencies students need is a critical first step in this process of defining the skills a coach needs. As I have noted previously, coaches believe that students need critical thinking, communication, and collaboration skills and to be more creative. They also recognize that traditional instruction won't help develop these skills. Their answer to the first question tells prospective coaches that they need to develop a range of skills to help other teachers improve teaching and learning.

After they complete this activity, prospective coaches understand that students need new skills and competencies but still wonder, "What does all this mean for me? What skills and competencies do I need to help my peers reshape and improve student learning?" As I worked with the team that created Peer Coaching, we repeatedly asked the question, "What skills and competencies do coaches need to be successful as they help their peers to improve teaching and learning?" Our answer is that successful coaching rests on the coach's use of three interrelated sets of skills.

Think of a successful coach sitting on the stool in Figure 3.1. The coach's success rests on her ability to utilize skills in all three areas: coaching skills (communication and collaboration), ICT (information and communication technology) integration, and lesson design. Remove any leg and coaching could fail. Let's begin to explore the kinds of skills coaches need now, and we will discuss each of these sets of skills in much more depth in subsequent chapters.

Coaching Skills: Communication and Collaboration Skills

Communication and collaboration skills are the keys to a coach's success. As we noted in Chapter 1, many teachers rarely collaborate with one another; instead they plan, teach, and rethink their practice alone. We learned that a coach's success depends on her or his ability to encourage peers to collaborate by forging a relationship with her or his learning partner that is based on respect and trust. What a coach says and does defines the coaching relationship and determines whether a peer trusts her coach. We also learned that a coach's success relies on his or her ability to create a safety net that

Figure 3.1   Key Coaching Skills

Source: Meyer et al. (2011t).

encourages the learning partner to take risks to improve teaching and learning. Both communication and collaboration skills are essential to build trust, respect, and the safety net.

A quick look at three sets of communication and collaboration skills should demonstrate their critical importance. First, if coaches want to avoid taking on the role of expert, they need to emphasize inquiry over advocacy. This means a coach needs to listen carefully, to raise questions that encourage the peer to think more deeply about the challenges he or she faces, and to ensure the peer plays an active role in defining solutions to the problems. In other words, the coach needs strong communication skills. Second, if the coach is really going to help the learning partner to build the capacity to improve teaching and learning, the coach needs to understand how to shape norms that ensure that both the coach and the learning partner are taking individual and collective responsibility for improving their practices as educators. Put another way, coaches need collaboration skills. Third, if a coach is going to be effective at observing a peer and offering feedback as they discuss what the coach saw and heard, a coach must know how to use communications skills and collaborative tools like protocols. Protocols structure the conversation and keep it focused on learning, not on the teacher.

Skills Gap. While we might assume that since teachers learn to provide feedback to students every day, they would have the skills to discuss teaching practice and offer feedback to colleagues. Evaluators of Peer Coach training in Montana found that participants did not feel that the skills they used with students translated to their work with other educators. As a result, they felt unprepared for meaningful collaboration with peers until they developed more communication and collaboration skills (Hanfling, 2011, pp. 5, 8). These educators were not unique. Few prospective coaches have any formal training to help develop these essential collaboration or communication skills. It is even more unusual to find prospective coaches that have experience using these skills with other educators. It isn't at all surprising that prospective coaches lack these skills. As Garmston and Wellman (1999) concluded, collaboration needs to be "structured, taught, and learned" (p. 18).

> Participants did not feel that the skills they used with students translated to their work with other educators. As a result, they felt unprepared for meaningful collaboration with peers until they developed more communication and collaboration skills (Hanfling, 2011, pp. 5, 8).

Lesson Design

If a Peer Coach's primary goal is to help a peer improve the quality of teaching and learning, it should be obvious that the coach needs effective lesson design and related pedagogical skills. This isn't just the coach's primary goal; it is a huge task. As we noted in Chapter 1, it is likely Peer Coaches will have to help peers engage students in learning that emphasizes skills like critical thinking and creativity. By itself this is a big goal, but one that advances in learning sciences make larger. In their seminal work *How People Learn*, John Bransford and his coauthors (2000) insist that "the emerging science of learning underscores the importance of rethinking what is taught, how it is taught, and how learning is assessed" (p. 13). Pretty breathtaking, right? Aside from lunch, the authors of this study insist every facet of what happens in traditional classrooms must change. While this research may or may not be familiar to coaches, they know that many of the teachers they coach will be attempting to undertake a fundamental improvement in potentially every facet of teaching and learning.

Skills Gap. My experience offering professional development to thousands of teachers over the last two decades has convinced me that many teacher leaders don't have a great deal of training or experience that would prepare them to help other teachers improve learning activities. Some prospective coaches may have had limited training designed to help them develop project-based learning activities. Most prospective coaches are innovators or early adopters. For them, the idea that students should be actively engaged in learning activities to solve problems with meaning to them outside the classroom stuck a responsive chord. They drew on these beliefs along with whatever training in lesson design they had and began experimenting with ways to put their pedagogical beliefs into practice in their classrooms. Only a handful of Peer Coaches have had extensive training in how to design learning activities as a result of participating in programs like Understanding by Design or Teaching for Understanding.

While they may have some personal experience with active, engaging learning strategies, few prospective Peer Coaches report that they have had any experience helping other teachers adopt similar learning practices or experience using processes or resources that would facilitate their efforts to coach another teacher. In this sense, they are like most of their peers. Darling-Hammond and colleagues (2009) found that American teachers have had "little professional collaboration in designing curriculum and sharing practices, and the collaboration that occurs tends to be weak and not focused on strengthening teaching and learning" (p. 5).

The innovative teachers discussed in Chapter 2 concluded that teachers need a highly skilled champion to support their efforts to adopt innovative practices in their classrooms. If coaches are to play this role, it is critical that coaches have lesson-design skills, processes, and resources to bring to their collaboration with their peers. It is also essential that coaches have at least some experience using these processes, resources, and skills before they enter a classroom to help a peer if we expect them to be successful.

ICT Integration

Finally, coaches need to acquire a deep understanding of the most promising practices in ICT integration so they can assist teachers in using technology to enrich and enhance student learning. Since there is little evidence that pairing technology with traditional didactic instruction will improve student learning, successful integration of technology means using this powerful learning tool in conjunction with active, engaging instructional strategies. In other words, successful integration of technology is inextricably linked directly to effective lesson design.

Over the years, I have been asked many times why technology integration is one of the three fundamental skills in a coaching program. At times it is hard to imagine why anyone would raise the question. I have been lucky enough to visit schools in many of the 40 countries in which I have trained Peer Coaches. I often ask students in these schools to name the tools most important to their learning. If they have access, they always include their cell phone, particularly text messaging, and the Internet. And they want to use these tools in school. In the 2007 *Speak Up* report, the authors noted, we have heard repeatedly and more strongly each year, students' discontent with school rules that limited their access to technology at school and rules that prohibit them from using at school the very technology tools and devices that they use constantly outside of school...in all aspects of their lives. (Speak Up, 2008, p. 7)

In a sense, students see educators as the barrier keeping them from using the learning tools most meaningful to them.

Increasingly, schools are weaving technology into teaching and learning. Curriculum standards for literacy and math in countries like Sweden, Australia, and the United Kingdom have long included the use of ICT. Until recently, technology wasn't woven into the curricular standards of many states in the United States, but the Common Core State Standards reflect the importance of educators using technology in daily learning. The K–5 Writing Standards, for example, call for students to, "with guidance and support from adults, use a variety of digital tools to produce and publish writing, including in collaboration with peers" (Common Core State Standards Initiative, 2011). The Common Core standards do integrate technology, not just for writing and communication but also across the curriculum for K–12 students. And they put a premium on classroom teachers who can guide and support students' efforts to use technology in the learning process.

There is another fundamental reason for technology integration to be one of the keystones of a coaching program. Technology is not only ubiquitous at work and at home; it has reshaped society and the economy. If the goal of educators is to prepare students for their future, teachers need to know how to use the same tools that working professionals in their fields use in the workplace. In *Preparing Teachers for a Changing World*, Bransford and Darling-Hammond (2005) insist that biology teachers need to know how to use probe ware, graphing calculators are a must for mathematicians, and history and social studies teachers need to know how to use a database to access, analyze, and synthesize data.

Technology integration is one of the three key skill sets a coach needs because it would be malpractice for a coaching program to train coaches and not arm them with the skills they need to help teachers integrate technology in ways that enrich and enhance learning.

Technology integration is one of the three key skill sets a coach needs because it would be malpractice for a coaching program to train coaches and not arm them with the skills they need to help teachers integrate technology in ways that enrich and enhance learning.

Skills Gap. Most of the coaches who enroll in Peer Coaching are innovators or early adaptors who have been successful at integrating technology in ways that enriched and enhanced learning. But when asked how they developed these technology-enriched learning activities, many noted that they saw or used some new technology, felt it was really cool, and looked for a way to reshape a learning activity around this new tool. In other words, they are acting on the assumption that technology drives improvements in teaching and learning. Michael Fullan (2011a) insists technology doesn't drive improvement. Smart pedagogy does. In short, coaches need to learn to use a process for integrating technology that:

- Starts with educational goals or standards
- Focuses next on content and pedagogy
- Explores if and how technology can support the tasks they are asking students to complete in ways that really enrich and enhance student learning

Content-Specific Training?

These three core skill sets do not include skills in any one content area or pedagogical skills related to specific content like history, math, or physics. Obviously there are coaching programs in literacy and math that put a priority on content-specific coach training. Is content-specific training essential? Schools choose teacher leaders to participate based on the needs and interests of the school. One of the first school districts we worked with chose to train teacher librarians from every school to be coaches, since they wanted to make coaching available to a broad cross-section of teachers. Another district chose only math teachers to become coaches. At a senior high school near Sydney, Australia, all six coaches at the school work with teachers who teach a different subject. Jenny Linklater, who coaches and supports all of the school coaches, says the school elected to have its Peer Coaches work with partners outside of their teaching area because they want differing perspectives, cross-curricular learning, and to "ensure it was not a mentoring situation where partners could rely on the expert knowledge of the coach" (J. Linklater, personal communication, June 14, 2012).

The operating assumption is that schools are choosing teacher leaders that meet the schools' needs and have the necessary content skills. Peer Coach training focuses on helping them to develop communication, lesson-design, and technology-integration skills they can apply when they coach peers in their schools no matter what content they are teaching. This agnostic approach has proven useful for Peer Coaches in K–12 classrooms no matter what content they teach.

Let's not be confused on this point. None of this discussion should suggest that coaches have all the preparation they will need when they finish coach training. They won't. Like any form of effective professional learning, training coaches needs to be long term and ongoing. Many coaches do go on to take additional training related to a specific content area or content-related pedagogy. And many coaches benefit from additional training designed to meet the unique needs of the student population of their school. We will explore how schools and school districts provide ongoing training for coaches that align with the needs of the school or district in Chapter 10.

Peer Coach Training at a Glance

Developing this core set of interrelated skills (communication and collaboration, lesson design, and technology integration) requires a significant investment of time and energy by prospective coaches and carefully focused training that helps them develop these skills in the context in which they will be used.

Highly Collaborative

Long before our small team created the training for Peer Coaches, two members of that team had years of experience leading professional development designed to help teachers create active, engaging, technology-rich learning activities. Our experiences could have provided evidence for the research on the value of collaboration. We saw the power of collaboration as we observed more than 1,000 teachers working together to improve student learning successfully, and we drew on this experience while creating the training for coaches. Collaboration is woven into the DNA of Peer Coaching.

> Collaboration is woven into the DNA of Peer Coaching.

Connected to Classroom Practice

Coach training is also designed to be closely connected to the coach's practice. Training is aligned with the work a coach does as he or she coplans learning activities with peers, models or team-teaches, and observes colleagues teaching, and then reflects afterward. Prospective coaches develop the skills necessary to carry out these roles in the context in which they will be used in their schools' classrooms. Coaches develop lesson-design skills by working with a partner to improve an activity that comes directly from their classroom or their school. This lesson-improvement process offers the perfect opportunity to help coaches practice and improve their collaboration and communication skills as they work together. Coaches also have numerous opportunities to sharpen these communication and collaboration skills when their facilitators ask them to work with other teams to coach them in ways to improve their learning activities.

Intensive, Sustained

Coaches do not learn communication skills needed to help another teacher improve learning activities by practicing these skills once or twice. Peer Coach training recognizes this fact and stretches over a 12- to 18-month span. This gives prospective coaches the chance to learn something, practice what they learned in a variety of contexts, make mistakes, and learn from them. The training is also designed so that it can draw on what Peer Coaches learn on the job. Their classroom experiences help them to understand how to put what they have learned about coaching into practice. These same experiences also raise many questions. To help coaches share their success and address the questions that come from on-the-job experiences, more than a third of the Peer Coach training occurs after they have significant classroom experience coaching. A coach's preparation doesn't end when training concludes. Peer Coaches routinely comment that the initial training they receive as coaches is just the start of their learning process.

Earlier in this chapter, we reviewed three questions that help coaches answer the overarching question, "What skills and competencies do I need to support my colleagues successfully?" Throughout their training Peer Coaches participate in reflective activities that ask them what they have learned that would help them answer this question and how they will apply that learning. Coaches don't stop using this reflective process when they complete Peer Coach training. They continue to use these questions to determine their unmet needs. Coaches look for coaching workshops, conferences, and coaching learning communities to collaborate with other experienced coaches in face-to-face or online settings to continue to develop their coaching skills.

Summary

Successful coaching requires careful training and preparation. Unprepared coaches are most likely to fail. Worse yet, bad coaching can actually cause educators to conclude that there is no value to coaching or collaboration.

- Coaches are teachers or teacher librarians who have classroom experience that gives them credibility in the eyes of their colleagues.
- Teacher leaders become coaches because they want the opportunity to collaborate with peers to improve learning in their classrooms. The desire to empower their peers to improve instruction is another significant reason teachers become coaches.
- Many prospective coaches understand that one of their key goals is to assist peers to improve the quality of student learning. This requires fundamental changes in what is taught, how it is taught, and how learning is assessed.
- Teacher leaders often feel uncomfortable as they begin their preparation to become coaches because they worry they don't have the skills needed to reach their goals.
- Coach training focuses on three closely interrelated sets of skills. Without a solid command of these skills, coaches could fail:
  - Communications and collaboration skills
  - Lesson-design skills
  - Promising practices in ICT
- Preparation for coaches needs to be:
  - Highly collaborative
  - Connected to classroom practice
  - Intensive and sustained, even long after the coaches complete their formal training as coaches
- Coaches understand the power of collaboration and seek out opportunities for ongoing collaboration with other coaches in both face-to-face settings and a variety of online environments.

4

The Coaching Plan

The knowledge gap is not about what good professional development looks like; it's about knowing how to get it rooted in the institutional structure of schools.

—Richard Elmore (2004)

Creating an effective professional-development program is critical to a school's efforts to build the capacity to improve teaching and learning. Over the past 20 years, I have worked with hundreds of schools, and only a handful have created and sustained effective professional-development programs. Most have not gotten far in their efforts to develop such a plan. I saw more evidence of this when I helped to facilitate a Birds-of-a-Feather discussion for more than 30 coaches at the 2012 ISTE conference. During the course of the discussion, several coaches, who came from schools across the United States, reported that they felt "overworked" and "stretched thin" and that their work was "unfocused."

The facilitator of the group asked for a show of hands of those coaches who felt the same way. Virtually every hand in the room went up. I asked these coaches to raise their hands if they had a Coaching Plan that addressed key issues like how coaching aligns with school or district goals, who the coach will collaborate with, and how the school will provide the resources coaches need to be successful. No one raised a hand. One participant asked if such a thing actually existed. When I heard this, it felt like déjà vu all over again.

As schools introduced significant numbers of computers into computer labs, libraries, and classrooms in the early 1990s, many school leaders asked their innovators and early adopters to help colleagues use technology in their classrooms. Few schools or districts provided training to help make these teachers successful. It was rare to see any significant effort to align their activities with their school goals. It was even more unusual to see schools provide any compensation, recognition, or institutional support for early adopters or time to do the work. Educational leaders watched in frustration as most of these teacher leaders burned out and chose to return to their classrooms, close the door, and work in isolation. Those of us who lived through this experience were determined to learn from our errors.

As I worked with the team that created Peer Coaching in 2001, this experience was still in my mind. One of the four goals of the program was to "Assist schools to build the capacity to meet their own professional development needs" (Meyer et al., 2011s). As we learned in Chapter 3, one step toward helping schools develop this collective capacity was to assist individual teacher leaders to acquire and hone the skills needed to coach colleagues. Developing individual capacity isn't enough. The school's staff needs to build its collective capacity, and one avenue to reach this goal is to harness a coach's ability to serve as a catalyst for improving teaching and learning. How does the school harness the coach's ability? One step was clear. The coach, his or her principal, and other key colleagues need to create a Coaching Plan. For many of the schools I have worked with, this Coaching Plan was also the first step toward creating and implementing an effective professional-development plan.

That Coaching Plan needs to address a few critical issues. How does coaching align with school or district goals? Who would the coach collaborate with? What were the roles and responsibilities for the coach and the teachers the coach worked with? How would the school measure the success of its coaching program? Finally, what resources would the school or district need to provide to support successful coaching?

Peer Coaches clearly understand the value of a Coaching Plan. As one Peer Coach noted, "It is important to develop a plan, even if you later discover what you need to change, adapt, embrace or abandon. The [Coaching] plan gives you forward momentum and direction, plus it's a vision" (Liston, Peterson, & Ragan, 2008, p. 29). A well-thought-out Coaching Plan can also ensure the school provides the institutional structure necessary to support coaching and expand its reach throughout the school over time. In the last chapter, we observed that a coach's success required the development of three sets of skills and pictured successful coaches sitting on a three-legged stool. That stool has to rest on something firm. The foundation it sits on is the Coaching Plan. Without a solid Coaching Plan, it is unlikely that coaching will succeed.

> A well-thought-out Coaching Plan can also ensure the school provides the institutional structure necessary to support coaching and expand its reach throughout the school over time.

IS COACHING RIGHT FOR YOUR SCHOOL?

Let's take a short detour before we take a deep dive into the Coaching Plan and how it can build capacity. It is important to take a step back and ask if coaching is a good fit for every school. The short answer to this question is "no." What we have learned from the experiences of schools that are implementing coaching and about effective professional development offers some insights into the culture of schools that are ready for coaching. Coaching is most likely to succeed in schools in which:

> The four most important choices districts that are adopting coaching face are:
>
> 1. Choosing the right schools
> 2. Choosing the right teacher leaders as coaches
> 3. Choosing the right teachers to collaborate with coaches
> 4. Defining how they will support and sustain coaches

- Educators act on their understanding that ongoing collaboration among teachers is essential to improve teaching and learning.
- Collaboration aimed at improving learning is led by teacher leaders who are supported by the school's leadership. Improvement comes when it is both bottom up and top down (Fullan, 2001, 2011b; Knight, 2011a; Mulford, 2003).
- School leaders must recognize the value of leadership coming from many levels in the school by empowering and supporting the work of coaches.
- Educators believe they are encouraged to innovate and take risks.

It is important for educators who are thinking of adopting coaching to understand that not all of these cultural traits need to be present at the time the school adopts coaching. If these traits don't develop during the early stages of implementing coaching, the school's coaches are likely to feel frustrated and powerless. If the school culture doesn't change over time, coaching is likely to be another short-lived educational experiment.

CREATING THE COACHING PLAN

Much of the first day of Peer Coach training centers on activities designed to help the coach and his or her principal create a Coaching Plan. Participants go through activities that help them understand how coaching aligns with what educators know about effective professional development, activities that help them define possible roles and responsibilities for the Peer Coach, and the key attributes of a successful Coaching Plan. Coaches and their principals finish the plan when they return to their school and have a chance to discuss it with other key stakeholders, particularly the teachers the coach collaborates with.

ELEMENTS OF THE COACHING PLAN

The coach and his or her principal use a template to create their Coaching Plan that raises a series of issues outlined below (Meyer et al., 2011f). In an effort to provide a bit more insight into effective planning, I have added some additional thoughts after each element of the plan.

Academic Focus

One key step to using coaching to build a school's capacity to improve is to align all of the coach's work with the school's and school district's educational goals. The Coaching Plan asks each school team to draft a goal for its coach's work that defines who the coach will work with, what the collaboration will focus on, and how coaching aligns with school and district goals. The graphic in Figure 4.1 is designed to help guide this process.

Collaborating Teachers

Peer Coaches generally choose to work with teachers in the same grade level or subject area. While this choice is easy for most coaches, the question of how many teachers they should collaborate with is more vexing. On one hand, new coaches are often ambitious and want to work with several teachers or even their whole grade-level team. But on the other hand, most Peer Coaches are full-time teachers, with clear limits on the amount of time they have for coaching.

Figure 4.1   What Is Your Coaching Focus?

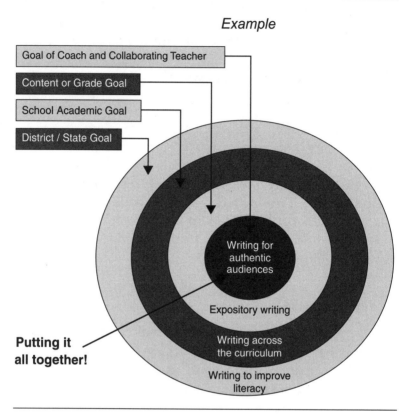

Source: Meyer et al. (2011f).

Experience and conversations with school or district leaders encourage these ambitious Peer Coaches to balance their ambition with the time available for coaching. Most coaches who are full-time teachers choose to collaborate initially with only one or two teachers. As we observed in Chapter 2, this doesn't limit the long-term impact of coaching. Success with one teacher can have a ripple effect that spreads coaching to include more teachers, even those who might have been resistant to the idea initially. As they get more experience, coaches often develop the skills and confidence to address this growing interest in collaboration.

As they develop their Coaching Plan, the coach and principal have to choose the right teachers to work with a coach, and the choice is critical. The first coaching experience needs to be successful if the school expects to sustain and expand the coaching program over time. If it isn't initially successful, coaching is off to a rocky start and may be doomed. So how does a coach choose the right teacher?

Three Models for Choosing a Collaborating Teacher

As I train facilitators, I routinely encourage them to tell their coaches to **start with the willing**. Recruiting a willing teacher is by far the most common model employed by new Peer Coaches. So how do we define what it means to be willing? Often this may mean the coach has a personal and professional friendship with the collaborating teacher, but being willing has to mean more than friendship. Jerker Porat, a Swedish Peer Coach, defined *willing* for us in its most basic terms: "I work with teachers who don't want to know" (J. Porat, personal communication, May 24, 2012).

> Jerker Porat, a Swedish Peer Coach, defined *willing* for us in its most basic terms: "I work with teachers who don't know but want to know."
> — J. Porat, personal communication, May 24, 2012

Porat and other successful coaches want some assurance that teachers they collaborate with are open to collaboration and want to improve teaching and learning. This willingness to collaborate and improve is essential. As Karen Soine, an instructional facilitator in Renton, Washington, notes, "Collaboration requires a growth mindset; a willingness to change and improve" (K. Soine, personal communication, June 5, 2012).

There are some literacy coaching programs in which the **principal assigns a teacher to work with a coach**. The coaches are there to help peers adopt a new practice and ensure the teacher is delivering the program with fidelity. This practice is extremely rare in Peer Coaching, because coaches know what their peer's reaction will be. Let's think for a minute about the simple litmus test for choosing a learning partner offered by Jerker Porat: Does this teacher "want to know"? Almost by definition, teachers who are assigned fail the test, because they don't want to know. Being assigned is just another way of saying they are forced into the coaching relationship. If they don't pass this test, Porat's response is clear. "I stay away from those who don't know and don't want to know." His response is typical of that of many other coaches. Why?

Teachers who are assigned to work with a coach have told me that they had the feeling that they must be doing something wrong. They believe there is something about their practice that needs to be fixed. It is unlikely that they will want to learn with and from someone assigned to help them. Knight's (2011a) research on instructional coaching led him to conclude that if teachers are assigned to work with a coach, they see it as punishment. It is hard to imagine a coach building a relationship of trust with a teacher who feels he or she is being punished and forced to change.

If a school has a full-time coach, it is quite common that the **coach would work with every teacher in the school.** If the coach is a full-time teacher, this model is rarely adopted because the coach rarely has the time or other resources to succeed. It did work for Melanie Hogan, a Peer Coach who was also a full classroom teacher, because of the creative approach she and her principal adopted. Her principal was optimistic the school's teachers would see the benefits of coaching and gave her a full day to meet with staff at her elementary school, just outside of Wollongong, Australia, to introduce Peer Coaching. After this introduction, Hogan was surprised when every one of the teachers said they wanted to be involved in Peer Coaching. To make the whole-school model work, Melanie asked the teachers to pair up and coach each other. Initially, their coaching emphasized observation and reflection. To facilitate their work, she taught key communication skills to all of the teachers and, over time, continued to help each of them to develop additional communication and collaboration skills. The fact that the principal saw the value of Peer Coaching, devoted budget to supporting coaching, and creatively found the time for teachers to observe each other and reflect afterward was also crucial to the success of this whole-school model (M. Hogan, personal communication, July 31, 2011).

Coach Roles and Responsibilities

As they develop their Coaching Plan, the coach, the principal, and the collaborating teacher define the five or six most important roles the coach will play. Any more than this and the coach's efforts may be spread too thin to be effective. As we noted in Chapter 1, these typically include coplanning learning activities, modeling or team-teaching, and observing peers and reflecting afterward. Knight's (2011a) work with instructional coaches led him to conclude that without agreement on roles, coaches are so often off task that some coaches "spend less than 25% of their time, often less than 10%...on coaching" (p. 99). While it is critical for the coach, the principal, and the collaborating teacher to agree on the Peer Coach's roles so the coach's work is focused, it is equally important for the collaborating teachers to define their roles so that they understand their responsibilities in the relationship. Both partners must understand and act on their individual and collective responsibilities for coaching to be effective at reaching its goals.

Norms

If coaching is going to help a teacher build capacity to improve teaching and learning, the coach and the learning partner must define and follow norms that will guide their collaboration. These norms may guide how they work together and help build trust and respect between the two. There is one norm that is critical to coaching success. This norm defines who owns the responsibility for learning. As we learned in Chapter 1, coaches can take on too many responsibilities and leave their partners in a state of learned helplessness. To ensure the teacher increases his or her capacity to create and implement effective learning activities, the coach and teacher need to establish a norm that recognizes the teacher and coach as peers and colearners. If the learning partner really wants to build capacity, the collaborating teacher must go one step further and agree to take responsibility for her or his own learning.

Resources

The resources required for successful coaching vary widely from school to school. If the coach is going to be freed to coach for half the day or the full day, there is a significant budgetary commitment. If the school is going to offer coaches a stipend, the school will have to provide the funding. In some cases, equipment, like technology, may be essential. Time is the one resource that is a constant in every Coaching Plan. It is the one commodity that is always in short supply in schools. Nearly 70% of the coaches surveyed in Washington State by Liston and Ragan (2010) found the absence of time to be a barrier—often a major barrier—to their work as coaches. Time may be in critically short supply, but creative school leaders and coaches can find the time.

> Time may be in critically short supply, but creative school leaders and coaches can find the time.

Peer Coaches report that many brief meetings with peers occur before school, in the hallway, at lunch, or after school. While these meetings provide just what the teachers need in a timely fashion, coaches and teachers also need longer blocks of time to plan lessons, analyze data, and reflect on instruction. Coaching Plans often identify the number of days a school dedicates to coaching, but the reality is that hours are a more effective unit of measurement. For coaches and the teachers they collaborate with, it is hard to get more than a couple of hours away from the classroom, and more importantly, educators involved in coaching argue that collaboration—whether it is coplanning an activity, modeling, or observation and reflection—works best in short blocks of time.

Many schools find time for coplanning and other coaching activities by reallocating time devoted to grade-level meetings, whole-school staff meetings, and established professional-development time to coaching activities. Secondary schools can provide time by rearranging teaching schedules or using block schedules so teachers have common planning times. This approach doesn't work terribly well in elementary schools where planning time is measured in minutes. Other schools have late starts or early-dismissal days built into their schedules and use this time for coaching.

Peer Coaches find that modeling, team-teaching, and observing a peer are powerful professional learning tools. But finding and providing time for these activities requires that schools make an additional commitment to coaching. Since observation can only occur while classes are in session, the schools need to find someone to take the classroom of the teacher who will be observing. Fortunately, effective observation can occur in an hour or less if the educators involved have a clearly defined sense of purpose and specific indicators of what they are looking for. Some schools use their budget for substitutes to provide time for these coaching activities; others eliminate after-school and weekend workshops and use this budget to fund the costs of substitutes for coaching-related work.

How much time does a coach need to collaborate with a teacher to be effective? The answer depends on the needs of the collaborating teacher and the skill and experience a coach brings to the relationship. The amount of time needed is also shaped by the simple fact that some teachers and coaches are much more effective collaborators than others. The team that created Peer Coaching wanted to know how much collaboration with a coach was required to produce real changes in teacher practice. When the program evaluators focused on one topic, technology integration, they found that 30 hours of collaboration produced increases in the teachers' use of technology with students. More significant changes in comfort and use with students occurred when the coaches collaborated more than 40 hours (Cohen & Patterson, 2006). These findings are roughly consistent with those of Darling-Hammond and colleagues (2009), who found that teachers typically need close to 50 hours of professional development to improve their skills and their students' learning.

Communication

Effective coaching aims at helping individual teachers develop the capacity to improve teaching and learning and to assist the school to develop the collective capacity necessary to improve teaching and learning based on the district and school goals and the needs of the students. Common interests, collaborative efforts, and capacity building all require effective communication between and among a school's educators. There are three key elements to effective communication among the coach, the principal, and other educators at the school.

> Common interests, collaborative efforts, and capacity building all require effective communication between and among a school's educators.

The first is that the principal, coach, and other educators at the school need to have an understanding of the value of coaching, what coaches do, and what coaching will look like at their school. One of the easiest ways to begin this process is for the principal to participate in the coach training session, where he or she works with coaches to start to create his or her school's Coaching Plan, then returns to the school to further refine the plan with input from collaborating teachers and other stakeholders. Principals who participate in shaping these Coaching Plans have a strong buy-in to coaching and are more willing to take the second step in effective communication.

If the goal of professional development is systemic change, then it is critical for the coach and principal to share their Coaching Plans with the whole school staff and—much like Melanie Hogan—help the staff understand how coaching supports the school's educational goals. Many coaches who have struggled to get support for their work as coaches tell me that they have not shared their Coaching Plan with their staff. They may be collaborating with one or two teachers, but without sharing their plan, they are barely one step from working in isolation. The principals and the entire staff need to know about coaching, how it will be implemented and assessed, and what it might mean for the school to win their buy-in and support.

The third element in effective communication is regular, ongoing communication among the coach, collaborating teachers, and school leadership. Many principals observe teachers and coaches coplanning a learning activity to get insights into how coaching is playing out in their schools. Effective communication also means routine meetings between the coach and the principal. Knight's (2011a) research shows that frequent meetings between the coach and principal were one key to success for the outstanding instructional coaches he studied. Many Peer Coaches understand the importance of updating their principal routinely and report they meet once or twice a month. The meetings are designed to keep the principal in the loop to help him or her understand what the coach and teachers are working on and its impact on teaching and learning. These same conversations can also focus on how coaching might grow to meet the broader professional-development needs of the school.

Coaches often use a collaboration log to track key information (see Figure 4.2) and as a powerful tool in conversations with their principals. Several years ago, Microsoft invited educators from across Latin America to a workshop to gain more insight into Peer Coaching. One activity gave them the chance to discuss coaching with a principal, coaches, and teachers from a school in the Edmonds School District. The first question the visiting educators asked the principal was "What do your coaches do?" The principal responded by saying that she had just reviewed her coaches' collaboration logs and went on to provide a short response that demonstrated enormous insight into the activities of her coaches and how their work supported school goals.

Coaches and principals need to be clear that the information shared in collaboration logs and meetings between coaches and their principals is part of an ongoing discussion about how coaching is meeting school needs but cannot be part of teacher evaluation. If the conversations are headed in that direction, coaches like Tracy Watanabe have found they "occasionally need to remind the principal that the coach's role is to promote innovation, not to fix anyone" (T. Watanabe, personal communication, May 22, 2012).

The three-part communication plan laid out above is the ideal, but practice doesn't always work in ways that are consistent with the ideal. I have seen examples in which coaches develop a Coaching Plan without sharing it and communication between Peer Coach and principal is rare. In these situations, principals may be generally supportive of coaching but lack any real understanding of the work done by the coach and his or her learning partner or the value of trying to expand coaching to meet school needs. Faulty

> The success of coaching as a tool for systemic schoolwide improvement is a function of communications among coach, the principal, and other educators in the school.

Figure 4.2   Collaboration Log

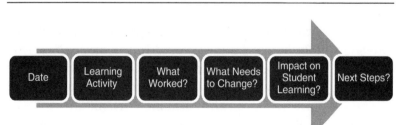

Source: Meyer et al. (2011g).

communication may mean coaching is on its way to becoming another small-scale, short-lived educational experiment. It is difficult to imagine coaching could realize its potential for systemic improvement without much stronger communication between the coach and the principal, who typically controls the budget and drives the school's educational agenda. The success of coaching as a tool for systemic schoolwide improvement is a function of communications among coach, the principal, and other educators in the school.

Aligning Professional-Development Efforts

In a day and age of dramatically shrinking educational budgets, school leaders must align all professional-development efforts to make their limited resources more effective. As we noted earlier, many schools rely on workshops and short-duration training for professional development. If the school wants to make these investments more effective, it needs to include a coach in the workshop to provide ongoing collaboration, support, and reflection for the educators who participate. Increasingly we are seeing schools with literacy coaches, math coaches, Peer Coaches, and more. All too often I have heard coaches report competition and even antipathy between the various coaching camps. To ensure alignment between various brands of coaching, the school principal needs to be certain that all the coaches are working for a common norm for effective learning and using consistent instructional strategies linked to that norm for learning. A Coaching Plan can also help in this process of aligning the work of these various coaches.

The Coaching Plan can and should help align Peer Coaching with any other capacity-building efforts in the school, like professional learning communities (PLCs). Peer Coaches can play and have played an important role in furthering the work of professional learning communities. Coaches have helped educators in New South Wales use communication skills in PLCs to improve the effectiveness of the group. Peer Coaches are also helping educators in learning communities use protocols, norms, and other collaborative skills to shape "discussions around teaching strategies, new ones, the kind of discussions that have been heated and unproductive in the past because of too much passion" (P. Cleaves, personal communication, May 23, 2012). Tracy Watanabe, a Peer Coach in Arizona, noted that one middle school department had a large number of coaches that helped peers to move from conversations that emphasized teaching to discussions focused on the learners. Teachers in this department recognized the difference. Prior to their work with coaches, PLC was a "bad word." Now teachers are saying, "Hey we are a PLC" (T. Watanabe, personal communication, July 8, 2011).

Measuring Progress

Coaching is like any other professional-development measure schools implement: It should be evaluated to determine if it is meeting its goals. If the school has been implementing for coaching a year or more and it isn't reaching the goals the school set, educators need to rethink how they are implementing coaching. This may mean collaborating with schools that have been more successful at implementing coaching. Schools use a variety of strategies to measure the success of Peer Coaching.

- Frequently, schools measure the success of Peer Coaching based on its impact on changing teacher practices.
- Schools might also measure teacher behavior and attitudes.
- They may ask teachers to reflect on how their teaching is different because of their work with a coach.
- Many schools review examples of lessons teachers used prior to coaching and lessons shaped after the coach and teachers worked together. This pre- and postanalysis focuses on whether Peer Coaches help teachers offer students more authentic, engaging learning activities, the kind that will help the students develop skills in critical thinking, collaboration, communication, and creativity.

- Some schools gather student work samples to see how their learning is changing as the coach and teacher collaborate over time.

Ultimately, after coaching is well established in a school and coaches have had the chance to collaborate with a wide number of teachers for some time, schools should be assessing their coaching program's effects on student learning.

COACHING PLAN: NEXT STEPS

What do you do with a Coaching Plan once it is complete? At the end of the first year of coaching, most coaches work with their learning partners and principals to revise it. One coach in Montana said, "The plan is a place to begin. It helps organize what you think you can do for another teacher. Once you begin, however, you need to be open to changing the plan so it evolves in response to changing needs" (Hanfling, 2011, p. 29). Changing needs are only part of the reason to revise the plan. The coaches have new skills and a wealth of experience after practicing their craft for a year. After reflecting on their experiences and growth in the past year, the coach, collaborating teachers, and principal are ready to revise the plan to move forward. Many schools reconsider the goals they outlined for coaching, some rethink how they measure coaching success, and most reconsider the resources they have devoted to coaching. One thing the principal and coach should be considering is what they can do to use coaching to expand the school's capacity to improve teaching and learning.

Building Capacity: Bringing Coaching to Scale

One simple way to expand the school's capacity is to increase the number of coaches in the school. This process is often a natural outgrowth of initial coaching successes. "Once a coach's learning partner has seen success," Phillippa Cleaves, a facilitator in New South Wales, Australia, observed, "they are willing to 'pay it forward' and share what they learned with the next wider circle of educators" (P. Cleaves, personal communication, May 23, 2012). This idea of "paying it forward" can be another form of the ripple effect we talked about in Chapter 2. An example of how paying it forward forms a ripple comes from an elementary school in Flagstaff, Arizona. In her first year of coaching, Maureen McCauley, a Peer Coach and library media specialist, worked with two teachers. They all met once a week to address the agenda they had created. During that first year, McCauley noted she could see that one of the second-grade teachers she was coaching "was sharing our conversations and ideas with another, nearby second-grade teacher" (Huston & King-George, 2010). While McCauley continued to work with her original collaborating teachers in her second year as a Peer Coach, she also began to collaborate with a grade-level team. Both of her original collaborating teachers continued to informally share what they learned from their collaboration with McCauley with others and went on to become Peer Coaches themselves. Routine revision to the Coaching Plan gives the school the opportunity to identify these examples of serendipitous growth and intentionally plan ways to capitalize on the ripple effect by asking successful collaborating teachers to pay it forward by engaging in formal training to become a Peer Coach.

One of the most important questions schools face as they revise their Coaching Plans is whether to move from a model in which the coach is collaborating with individual teachers to one in which the coach, like McCauley, is working with a grade-level team or a content team. There are challenges to this model, particularly the amount of time needed to expand the coach's circle, but there are also clear advantages. Having a coach work with all of the fourth-grade teachers could mean that all of the teachers work collectively to bring their ideas for effective learning into classroom practice by coplanning learning activities that all of the members of the group would use. In addition to sharing resources, the group can choose to focus on developing its skills in a specific area like formative assessment. The group would work with the coach to learn more about this ongoing assessment strategy and apply what it learned in all of its classrooms. The power of observation and reflection also grows if the grade-level or subject team members are all participating. These reflective discussions not only help the team define where it needs to improve collectively but also give the teachers clear ideas of what help they need from a coach to improve their practices.

Whether a coach is working with others who teach at her grade level, a subject-matter team, or all of the colleagues at her school, the school's educators are developing collective capacity to improve teaching and learning. Schools build this capacity, Fullan (2011b) believes, by "developing collaborative, focused cultures at the school level; a new role for the principal as lead learner and supporter; the identification of lead teachers to play a supportive and collaborative role among peers" (p. 38). I think we need to add one element to Fullan's equation. Schools also build this capacity through careful planning over time. Looking at it from a slightly different perspective, then, we can see that the Coaching Plan does more than guide the school to develop the capacity to meet its professional-development needs; it can also be a key element in helping the school to develop the collective capacity essential to improving teaching and learning.

> The Coaching Plan does more than guide the school to develop the capacity to meet its professional-development needs; it can also be a key element in helping the school to develop the collective capacity essential to improving teaching and learning.

There is one last step each school needs to take with its Coaching Plan. While there is clear value to creating and revising a Coaching Plan as the school launches its coaching program, the value of having a Coaching Plan that is separate from the school's strategic plan quickly diminishes over time. Once it is clear that a school understands what is necessary to support and expand its coaching efforts, the Coaching Plan needs to be woven into the school's strategic plan. At this point, the school is taking what it has learned about effective professional development and building it in to the institutional structure of the school.

Summary

Coaching Plans help schools utilize limited human infrastructure, the school's teacher leaders. Effective Coaching Plans ensure that the coach and her or his learning partner have the support, resources, and guidance coaching needs to successfully meet the needs of the school.

- Communication is critical to the success of coaching. Effective communication rests on:
  - The principal's participation, along with that of the coach and collaborating teachers, in shaping the Coaching Plan
  - Communicating the plan to the school staff
  - Coaches who routinely update their principals on coaching activities and engage in discussions about how coaching is meeting the school's needs and the next steps for coaching
- Without effective communication, coaching might be another small-scale, short-term educational experiment.
- Effective schools revise their Coaching Plan routinely so that it focuses on further developing the school's capacity to provide its own professional development and at the same time enhances the school's collective capacity to improve teaching and learning in every one of the school's classrooms.
- Once coaching is clearly established, successful schools weave the Coaching Plan into their school's strategic plan.

5

Communication
and
Collaboration

How teachers talk to one another is an essential resource of strong schools.

—Garmston & Wellman (1999)

Since successful coaching rests on three sets of skills—communication and collaboration, lesson design, and technology integration—many educators have asked if one of these skills is more important than the others. It is a question I have asked hundreds of Peer Coaches over the years, and they consistently respond that communication and collaboration skills are a prerequisite to successful collaboration.

A coach's successes in incorporating lesson-design skills and insights into the effective use of technology "hinge on their success with communication and collaboration skills" (J. Linklater, personal communication, June 14, 2012).

Jenny Linklater, a successful Australian Peer Coach, insists a coach's successes in incorporating lesson-design skills and insights into the effective use of technology "hinge on their success with communication and collaboration skills" (J. Linklater, personal communication, June 14, 2012). Virtually every coach I have spoken to echoes this argument. Why are communication and collaboration skills so important for coaches?

The goal of coaching is to produce the kind of strong, collaborative relationships between coach and learning partner that can improve student learning. Collaboration requires that coaches and their peers are learning with and from each other as they coplan learning activities, model, team-teach, observe, and reflect. This is a collaborative relationship that requires meaningful discussions about ways to improve teaching and learning, and these discussions are likely to challenge current practices and long-held beliefs. While the topic is professional, the questioning can seem personal. To improve teaching and learning, these challenging conversations need to be an ongoing part of the relationship between the coach and their learning partners.

Most Peer Coaches I have worked with know that they are trying to build these kinds of relationships in difficult circumstances. Many have worked in schools in which teachers work alone and in which collaboration consisted of teachers exchanging lesson plans and teaching resources. Let me give you an example of what collaboration in this environment could look like. For 7 years, I led a professional-development program that offered teams of teachers from school districts across western Washington 5 days of training on a university campus. While in residence, they learned about project-based learning and integrating technology to enhance learning and created a classroom-ready learning activity that applied what they learned. Collaboration was the driving force in the creation of these learning activities, but it wasn't always successful. Tensions between learning partners were common; several times each summer these tensions boiled over into conflicts. The teachers involved told me they could no longer work with or share a dorm room with their partner; they wanted a divorce. These educators had no real experience they could draw on to defuse differences of opinion, and the training didn't help them develop collaboration skills. Disagreements that frequently started over pedagogy became personal in nature. These experiences aren't unique.

Peer Coaches may not know Kise's (2012) research that identifies the lack of collaboration skills as one of the three barriers that keep groups of educators from working together effectively, but they have often seen staff discussions over new teaching strategies founder as these conversations turned personal, emotional, and ugly. Previous experiences have convinced Peer Coaches that they need strong communication and collaboration skills to make collaboration with their peers effective.

COLLABORATION NEEDS TO BE
"...STRUCTURED, TAUGHT, AND LEARNED"

Since teachers and coaches have worked largely in isolation, they have had little reason or opportunity to develop strong collaboration or collaboration skills. My experience in working with Peer Coaches led me to the same conclusions drawn by Garmston and Wellman: "collaboration needs to be taught and learned" (1999, p. 18). These aren't the kinds of skills that educators pick up intuitively. Communication and collaboration skills must be taught in carefully structured activities and repeatedly practiced in the context in which Peer Coaches will use them in their schools. Learning them is the easy part. Applying them in a variety of classroom settings and using them effectively is much more difficult. We will explore some strategies to help coaches develop these skills in this chapter as we discuss some of the communication and collaboration skills that are vital for successful Peer Coaching.

Meeting Norms

In Chapter 4, we touched on the importance of having the Peer Coach and his or her collaborating teacher establish norms to guide their relationship. Let's take a closer look at the value of norms. Almost any group that functions effectively has established group norms to guide conduct during meetings. These group norms are designed to keep meetings productive and focused. If there were Robert's Rules for effective meetings, these types of norms would be included:

- Begin and end on time
- Silence and put away cell phones
- Stay on agenda
- Do assignments prior to meetings
- Observe basic conversational courtesies
- Monitor your own airtime
- Avoid side conversations (Meyer et al., 2011r)

Another type of norm that effective groups adopt is designed to minimize conflict by keeping conversations focused on the issues being considered. This kind of norm also offers groups a way of holding each member accountable for actions and performance. Norms that have these goals might include:

- Hold yourself personally accountable
- Listen respectfully
- Discuss issues, not people
- Show respect for views of others
- Assume positive intentions (Meyer et al., 2011r)

Peer Coaches get their first experience with norms when they establish the norms their group will follow through their coaching training. Each training cohort of prospective coaches suggests norms to guide the group's work and explain why they believe their norms would be valuable for the group to adopt. After discussion, Peer Coach trainers ask the group to pick five or six to guide the group's actions (Meyer et al., 2011r).

Many people have told me they see the value of norms but wonder how to hold people accountable to them. To be effective, groups need to do much more than create a set of norms and file them away. Norms need to be an integral part of every meeting. To model this behavior for prospective coaches, their trainers, called facilitators, start every training session by reviewing the group's norms to remind the group of their commitment. At the end of each session, they ask the Peer Coaches for specifics on how the norms guided the group's work. If they haven't been too successful in following the norms, the facilitator is likely to ask what they could do differently the next time. Since norms aren't carved in stone, facilitators also ask the group if they need to revise their list of norms to make the group more effective (Meyer et al., 2011r). Each of these activities is designed to ensure that Peer Coaches understand the value of norms and how norms can guide their collaboration with colleagues in their schools.

Collaborative Norms

The second set of meeting norms we just reviewed is closely related to another type of norms, which Garmston and Wellman (1999) call collaborative norms. Collaborative norms shape our conversations in ways that build trust and respect; they define accountability and build capacity. Collaborative norms are essential for effective coaching. In the first chapter, we talked about the ways coaches established coaching relationships that were personalized, friendly, manageable, private, and supportive. If you think about norms that encourage discussions of ideas instead of people, show respect for the ideas of others, and assume positive intentions, it should be fairly clear how these norms build the kind of relationship essential to successful coaching.

> Collaborative norms shape our conversations in ways that build trust and respect; they define accountability and build capacity. Collaborative norms are essential for effective coaching.

When we discussed how coaches make a learning partner feel supported in Chapter 1, we noted that it is easy for a coach to cross the tipping point and take responsibility for learning away from her or his peer. Effective coaches, like Grace Dublin, make it clear to learning partners that "the responsibility to learn something belongs to the learner" (G. Dublin, personal communication, September 13, 2011). When teachers come to a coach to discuss an issue they are grappling with, the coach helps them puzzle it out. There is some joint accountability. Jim Knight's (2011a) research on instructional coaching led him to conclude that joint accountability is an essential element of successful partnerships (p. 30). While joint accountability is important, ultimately the collaborating teacher develops the answer that he or she brings back to the classroom to implement. The teacher has drawn on what he or she learned with and from the coach and taken that learning to shape a solution. Think about the comparison we made earlier between coaching and teaching climbing. Coaches need to understand that their learning partners are just like people learning rock climbing: They need to be able to act on their own when they reach the crux of the problem.

Aspiring climbers don't need a norm that holds them responsible, but holding yourself accountable is a significant part of the equation that produces professional growth and success for educators. A number of researchers have observed that long-term collaboration focused on a single goal, like working to implement an explicitly agreed-on model for effective learning, produces a sense of internal accountability among peers. Educators who have had this kind of experience don't need external accountability to encourage them to improve; their commitment to one another to reach their common goals is a much more effective type of accountability (Elmore, 2004; Mourshed, Chinezi, & Barber, 2010). My experience suggests this form of accountability is more likely to develop if coaching pairs explicitly commit to norms that define their individual and collective

> Accountability is more likely to develop if coaching pairs explicitly commit to norms that define their individual and collective responsibilities for learning as they work together to improve student learning.

responsibilities for learning as they work together to improve student learning. Collaborative norms are part of the equation that builds a teacher's capacity to improve.

COMMUNICATION SKILLS

The list of communication skills effective peer coaches should master seems a bit overwhelming. It could include tone of voice, negotiating skills, choosing the right words to empower and motivate, facial expression, body language, and other dialogue skills. While the list of skills is lengthy, there is a very clear starting point for the development of these skills, and for Peer Coaches, that is the development of a handful of communication skills. Peer Coach training focuses on four key skills, three of which come from Garmston and Wellman's (1999) norms of collaboration and the last from other related resources. Prospective coaches get repeated practice using these four skills in a variety of settings like those the coaches will find in their schools. In addition to repeated practice, experience has proven that coaches develop these skills more effectively if the learning exercises include opportunities for participants to provide feedback to their peers, feedback that is designed to help coaches be more effective at using these communication skills.

Active Listening

If a coaching relationship is going to be personalized, coaches have to understand their learning partner's needs, interests, experiences, and perceptions. Active listening is one skill that promotes this kind of understanding. Active listeners are focused on what the speaker is saying. They look right at the speaker, block out competing thoughts, and assess what the speaker is saying. Looking right at the speaker may mean that active listeners lean in slightly to focus their attention on the speaker. Body language is important. Like many coaches, I have learned that facial expressions are an important part of listening. If coaches look bored or unhappy about what they are hearing, they are unlikely to have a strong, trusting relationship. Effective active listeners also understand that listening is understanding the speaker's needs, not an opportunity to share some personal experience about how they dealt with a similar situation. Listeners certainly don't interrupt with "Oh!! Oh!! Oh!!!!!" and then tell their story. If you're really good at listening, you let the speaker finish and then pause and reflect briefly before responding (Wellman, 1999; Meyer et al., 2011k).

Paraphrasing

In its simplest form, paraphrasing is the listener repeating, albeit in a modified form, what he or she heard the speaker say. I have talked to many educators who feel paraphrasing is little more than parroting and see it as insulting. At best, they feel it is waste of time. In reality, paraphrasing is one of the most important communication skills. Several years ago, I heard a speaker highlight the importance of paraphrasing when he said, "If you are interested in influencing action, what counts is what is heard—not what you said" (L. Foltos, personal notes from Global Integrity Leadership Group Workshop, 2008). Paraphrasing lets the listeners determine if they understand what the speaker meant. Paraphrasing is so effective at checking for understanding that we often see it used in critical, sometimes lifesaving situations. The next time you fly, listen to the pilots communicating with ground control. After the ground controller gives a command on altitude, speed, or heading, the pilot always repeats it. Why? What is important is not what is said but what is heard. How will the speaker know what is heard unless the listener repeats it?

> How will the speaker know what is heard unless the listener repeats it?

Paraphrases are designed to focus on the speaker and his or her ideas, so effective paraphrases don't include the pronoun *I*. Coaches avoid this pronoun because its use indicates that the speaker's ideas aren't important and the conversation is shifting to focus on the coach's ideas. It takes a lot of time and practice just to take the *I* out of paraphrases. One way to avoid this pronoun is to begin paraphrases with sentence stems like the following:

- "You are suggesting..."
- "You're proposing..."
- "So what you are thinking is..." (Garmston & Wellman, 1999, p. 40, in Meyer et al., 2011k)

Clarifying Questions

Clarifying questions are simple and typically factual. They fill in the missing pieces of the puzzle. A teacher may be describing some work he had groups of students complete. The listener may want to know: How many students were in each group? Did each member of the group have the same assignment? Was each group using the textbook or other resources for its work? Clarifying questions are typically easy to answer, and the answers are often short. They may be easy to ask and answer, but clarifying questions are important for the listener to have the full picture of the situation her colleague is describing (Meyer et al., 2011k).

Probing Questions

Probing questions are the tools coaches rely on if they really want to encourage their learning partners to solve the issues facing them. Why are they so critical? The answer gets to the heart of effective coaching. In Chapter 1 and earlier in this chapter, I noted that coaches strive to make their learning partners feel like they are supported, but Peer Coaches can't be the experts with the answers. Instead, as Grace Dublin insists, coaches are there to "help them formulate their strategies. It is ultimately their answer" (G. Dublin, personal communication, September 13, 2011). Probing questions are designed to get the teacher to think more deeply about and develop answers to the issues important to him or her. Probing questions give teachers a different perspective that helps them draw alternative conclusions on how to approach a problem. They are at the core of the inquiry method of learning and build the collaborating teacher's capacity to create and offer students powerful learning activities.

So what makes a good probing question? First, it must be a question. This may seem obvious, but many people who use probing questions already have an answer in mind when they ask the question. If the questioner knows the answer he wants, he is simply masking his solution with a question mark. Those who already have an answer in mind might as well ask, "Why don't you just do it the way I do?" At least that is a question. The National School Reform Faculty has an excellent *Pocket Guide to Probing Questions*. It recommends that the questioner start by determining if "you have a 'right' answer in mind. If so, delete the judgment, or don't ask it" (Thompson-Grove, Frazer, & Dunne, n.d.).

Effective probing questions usually start with a paraphrase, and they are often open ended. Stems or sentence starters might include the following:

- You said…; have you ever thought about…?
- Why…?
- What might the next step be?
- Are there other strategies that you could use to…? (Meyer et al., 2011k)

Don't underestimate these questions because they seem so simple. One of the most powerful probing questions I have heard is also one of the simplest. "So you tried…with your students. What did you learn from that?" Or the question might be asked a slightly different way. "So you tried… with your students. What did they learn from that, and what is your evidence?" Remember, the purpose of the probing question is to get the teachers to think more deeply about their practice. Simple probing questions can be incredibly powerful reflective tools.

Coaches aren't the only ones who benefit from communication skills. As Phillippa Cleaves, one of the directors of the Peer Coaching program in New South Wales, visits schools participating in Peer Coaching, she has seen teachers who learned these communication skills from a coach turn around and teach these same skills with their students (P. Cleaves, personal communication, May 23, 2012). If strong communication is one of the keys to 21st-century learning, these teachers are helping students develop communication skills to better prepare them for their futures.

Inquiry Over Advocacy

Probing questions are the key to inquiry-based learning and are essential for Peer Coaches who want to avoid advocating for a solution based on their ideas and experiences. I still smile when I think of the most egregious case of advocacy I have heard. Teachers from several countries were discussing the value of engaging the students in problem solving when one of them said, "Why should we waste time having students explore and solve problems? Teachers can tell them what they need to know. In my math classroom a circle is a circle unless I tell students it's a square!!!" (L. Foltos, personal notes, 2005). Experienced Peer Coaches know instinctively that this sort of advocacy would destroy a coaching relationship, but they wonder how often they can advocate a solution. When is the right time for advocacy? How often can they present their solutions? As I noted in earlier chapters, successful coaches feel that a little advocacy works, but only after a strong coaching relationship based on inquiry is formed. Too much advocacy, they observed, means the coach becomes the expert with the answer. Garmston and Wellman (1999) argue it is important for successful collaboration to balance advocacy and inquiry. Effective Peer Coaches emphasize inquiry over advocacy. Too much advocacy can produce learned helplessness. Inquiry builds capacity to improve teaching and learning by helping teachers to be more effective at designing and implementing learning activities that meet the needs of their students.

DEVELOPING COMMUNICATION
AND COLLABORATION SKILLS

Peer Coach training asks prospective Peer Coaches to participate in a number of activities designed to help them learn to use these communications skills. The first of these asks Peer Coaches to listen to a conversation between a coach and a collaborating teacher, to identify which communications skills were used by the coach, and to reflect on the value these skills brought to this conversation. Another activity is designed to give them practice paraphrasing. Coaches also practice using active listening, paraphrasing, and asking clarifying and probing questions while working in small groups using the National School Reform Faculty's probing question exercise. One valuable aspect of this exercise is that all of the listeners give the speaker a probing question related to the issue he or she raised. The speaker considers all the questions and then tells the group which probing question caused him or her to think the most deeply about his or her dilemma. This step gives those who raised probing questions direct and immediate feedback on what makes an effective probing question, feedback they can use as they develop and ask probing questions in the future (Dowd & D'Anieri, n.d., in Meyer et al., 2011k).

Conducting a Planning Meeting

Peer Coaches feel their first meeting with the collaborating teacher is critical to their efforts to personalize their relationship and ultimately to their success coaching this teacher. Jenny Linklater, a Peer Coach at a school outside of Sydney, and her school's coordinator of the Peer Coach program feel these first conversations "were an important first step in establishing trust and letting out the flood of ideas and experiences before we could focus on establishing firm goals and commencing focused coaching cycles" (J. Linklater, personal communication, June 14, 2012). Other Peer Coaches maintain that these initial meetings are critical because they establish the collaborating teacher's belief that working with a coach will help the teacher address his or her needs. In other words, they offer some proof of the value of collaborating with a coach. What we know from the learning sciences supports these coaches' belief about the value of the first meeting in personalizing their coaching relationship. Bransford, Brown, and Cocking (2000) argue that effective learning environments are learner centered and draw on students' current knowledge, skills, beliefs, passions, and culture (pp. 23–24). This idea of learner-centered education doesn't lose meaning or value because the learners are professional educators. And successful coaches act on this understanding.

Since these first meetings are so critical, Peer Coach training helps the prospective coaches prepare for this meeting by asking them to role play so they can understand how to shape the meeting using a planning worksheet that focuses the conversation on the school's academic goals, defining a focus for their coaching work, and discussing possible teaching activities that the coaching pair might focus on initially. The role-playing activity also gives coaches practice using the communications skills they are likely to use in this first meeting (Meyer et al., 2011i). Prospective coaches are awkward during these exercises, but with enough practice and experience, coaches might not even be conscious that they are using these communication skills. Shona Brooks, a Peer Coach at Silverton Primary School near Melbourne, Australia, told me that she wasn't sure she used probing questions. Catherine Ham, who was one of Shona's collaborating teachers, quickly interjected that Shona used them frequently and provided several recent examples of probing questions (S. Brooks and C. Ham, personal communication, August 3, 2011).

MOVING FROM NICE TO INNOVATION

As a group, educators are some of the nicest people in the world, but as Elisa MacDonald (2011) points out in her article "When Nice Won't Suffice," niceness isn't always a good quality, particularly if the goal is to encourage teachers to adopt innovative practices. Nice teachers observe each other and provide polite comments that emphasize what they appreciated about their colleagues' teaching, but MacDonald insists they avoid anything that seems judgmental, and "rarely question each other's...practice, assumptions and beliefs" (p. 46). City, Elmore, Friarman, and Teitel (2009) observed that "nice" teachers talk about how well the teacher's lesson went rather than focusing on student learning. These teachers may be seen by their peers as nice, but their comments are not likely to cause any deep reflection on teaching practice or encourage teachers to adopt innovative practices. We all know nice teachers. Our schools are full of them.

MacDonald hits right at the heart of what seems like a lovely little dichotomy that all Peer Coaches face. Many coaches believe that personal and professional friendship is key to their success. When you watch them coach, they are genuinely nice. On the other hand, the coach's job is to encourage innovation and improvement in teaching in learning. How do Peer Coaches resolve this dichotomy? They don't see the problem because they have redefined the term *nice*.

Coaches are friendly, supportive, positive, and constructive. These qualities help the coach build a safety net that is critical to success. Jenny Linklater, a Peer Coach who supports five other coaches in her school, insists that without the safety net and the "high-quality environment" of trust it creates, the coach's partner "will retreat to what is safe and easier or what has worked before" (J. Linklater, personal communication, June 14, 2012). In other words, supportive, positive, constructive behavior is a prerequisite to making the coach's learning partner feel safe to move out of his or her comfort zone. "Nice" behavior that helps build this safety net is an essential first step that opens the door and allows the coach to use the kind of probing questions that lead his or her

> Coaches define themselves as friendly and supportive peers who question teaching practices and encourage partners to take manageable risks to improve their practice. This is a long way from the definition of *nice* we described earlier.

learning partners to rethink their practice and to take risks by adopting innovative practices. Coaches define themselves as friendly and supportive peers who question teaching practices and encourage partners to take manageable risks to improve their practice. This is a long way from the definition of *nice* we described earlier.

Removing the Fear Factor

Let's look at an example of how an effective coach can play a role in promoting innovation. Teri Calsyn is a former kindergarten teacher who has been a Peer Coach for more than 8 years. When I asked Teri what she does to encourage innovation, the first words out of her mouth were, "It takes time" (T. Calsyn, personal communication, June 12, 2012). It takes time, she continued, because the coach needs to form a personal and professional relationship with his or her peer. "You have to laugh with them, commiserate with them, and encourage that teacher to define their goals for coaching" (T. Calsyn, personal communication, June 12, 2012). One of her first goals in building this relationship is to get to "we." Calsyn consciously works to use the pronoun *we* when collaborating with a teacher to create common ownership for learning, because it is a prerequisite to encourage a teacher to adopt an innovative teaching practice. Calsyn said she feels she needs to "get down and dirty" with her learning partners. "I can't be at the bottom of the cliff encouraging them to jump. I have to be willing to hold their hand and jump with them" (T. Calsyn, personal communication, June 12, 2012).

So what does "hand holding" and "getting down and dirty" entail? For Calsyn, it starts with coplanning and getting the teacher she is working with to define what he wants the students to get out of the learning activity. Hand holding typically means that Calsyn team-teaches with a peer so he has the time to observe Calsyn. At times, team-teaching serves a more important function. As Calsyn noted, "I am not afraid to let them see me fail" (T. Calsyn, personal communication, June 12, 2012). Finally, hand holding means debriefing after team-teaching or observing the peer teach. Calsyn always asks her peers to discuss what worked and what the peer would do differently next time.

While Calsyn works hard to emphasize what "we" are doing when she works with a peer, there is one clear exception to this. At the end of any planning session, she leaves her peer with a very clear statement of the next steps the teacher needs to take and makes it clear that these are the teacher's responsibility. Calsyn knows that there may be a finite amount of time she can coach a peer, so it is critical to her that her colleagues take responsibility for their own learning.

By this point, you are probably asking, if the teacher sets the goals for the collaboration, what happens if these goals have nothing to do with innovation? How does this kind of relationship ever lead to innovation? Calsyn (T. Calsyn, personal communication, June 12, 2012) says she supports the teacher's goals but is willing to push him. Pushing teachers doesn't mean she is trying to make them uncomfortable or that Calsyn is confrontational. Instead, she may build on a success they just had with a literacy activity in small-group settings. As they are debriefing the activity and planning next steps, Calsyn may suggest they try a slight twist on what they have done. If they are working on literacy, the twist may be that she asks the teacher about the value of creating a project that more actively engages students by asking them to take pictures, write a script, and create a photo story about some topic that has meaning in the students' lives. In other words, Calsyn is suggesting the next logical small step for the teacher to take. Throughout this process of nudging, pushing, and challenging her peers to take the next step, Calsyn wants her collaborating teachers to know they won't have to take the next step alone. To her, it's critical that she always maintains the "we" in relationships with her learning partners. While one might quibble about whether the coach is supporting the collaborating teacher's initial goals after the teacher has embraced several of these nudges and twists, Calsyn has been successful in helping the teacher to adopt more innovative teaching strategies.

Safety Net

Other successful Peer Coaches have followed some of the same strategies Calsyn uses, and there are two common traits in their work. Their efforts to encourage their peers to adopt more innovative teaching and learning strategies are always undergirded by the safety net they built with their collaborating teachers. Alessio Bernadelli explains this approach in unmistakable language when he argues that the coach must be as "supportive as you can be. Go the extra mile for them. When they trust you, you can push a bit" (A. Bernadelli, personal communication, May 23, 2012).

> Their efforts to encourage their peers to adopt more innovative teaching and learning strategies are always undergirded by the safety net they built with their collaborating teachers.

Small Changes: Continuous Improvement

Second, like Calsyn, successful Peer Coaches don't push for one big, dramatic change, instead relying on an incremental process of continuous improvement. These successful coaches insist that effective coaching requires an understanding of what people need, when they can do more and when they simply can't. In addition to keeping the workload manageable for their peers, successful coaches are careful to ensure that they aren't pushing their learning partners too far beyond the comfort level. This careful reading of their learning partners' needs encourages many coaches to work toward small changes and continuous improvement.

> Successful Peer Coaches don't push for one big, dramatic change, instead relying on an incremental process of continuous improvement.

Phillippa Cleaves, one of the managers of the Peer Coaching program in New South Wales, sees many Peer Coaches who have embraced this "start small" approach and argues there are long-term benefits to starting small. "Small successes ultimately have greatest impact," according to Cleaves. "Teachers need to see successes in things before they are willing to invest in it" (P. Cleaves, personal communication, May 23, 2012). Cleaves's comment hits on something I have observed while talking to Peer Coaches and their learning partners. The most likely avenue to get teachers to buy in to and implement a new vision for teaching and learning is to help them have some personal success implementing that vision in their classrooms with their students. With this success, teachers are more willing to take the next step to make that vision a reality in their classrooms.

Hopefully, by this point, you're thinking these Peer Coaches are creating the kind of manageable relationship described in Chapter 1. So what are some strategies successful Peer Coaches use to nudge, twist, and push?

Recognition

Successful Peer Coaches use a variety of strategies to get teachers recognition for their work. Many coaches use conversations with their peers to recognize the strengths of the learning activities the teachers are using with students and work to help their learning partners build on those strengths. By being supportive and recognizing what is already working, coaches can get their learning partners ready for some manageable risk taking. Several Peer Coaches encourage teachers to share their work—their successful learning activities—across the school and to blog to share their work with others beyond their school. The recognition teachers can get from sharing their work can build their confidence and encourage more innovation. If teachers won't toot their own horns, some coaches, like Tracy Watanabe, blog about what they see and learn in the classrooms of teachers who are collaborating with Peer Coaches.

Recognition doesn't have to come from those outside the school for it to be effective. Peer Coaches in Watanabe's district added "student successes and celebrations" as a new category in their collaboration log. Watanabe believes this small change offers the coach and teacher the opportunity to share evidence of successes and to celebrate, and it serves as a tool that encourages more innovation (T. Watanabe, personal communication, May 22, 2012).

Model Risk Taking

Other Peer Coaches model risk taking and recognize that taking risks may occasionally mean failure. David Macleod-Jones, a Peer Coach and an assistant principal at a senior high school outside Sydney, encourages teachers he coaches to take risks. To walk the talk, he asks them to help him improve a learning activity he had created and used with students (D. Macleod-Jones, personal communication, June 29, 2012). Tracy Watanabe models learning activities, and in the reflection that follows, she is explicit in pointing out risks she was taking (T. Watanabe, personal communication, May 22, 2012). John Albert, a principal and Peer Coach in Flagstaff, Arizona, encourages his learning partners by pointing out failures he has had in similar situations (J. Albert, personal communication, December 13, 2011).

Challenging Probing Questions

Mary Lou Ley, who directs the Wisconsin Peer Coaching Collaborative, encourages risk taking and innovation by putting even more emphasis on a tool Peer Coaches already use, probing questions. Ley (2011) insists that "professional growth occurs when we engage in focused conversations around evidence of teaching and learn-

> Professional growth occurs when we engage in focused conversations around evidence of teaching and learning.
> —Ley (2011)

ing." She acts on this belief by offering Peer Coaches exercises designed to prepare them to ask their learning partners more challenging probing questions by focusing on evidence of what the teacher intended and what the student learned (Ley, 2011).

As she encourages Peer Coaches to push for innovation, Ley (2011) is clear to remind them that there are boundaries to how hard they can press. Probing too hard can be counter-productive. To help make this point, Ley uses a graphic from the National School Reform Faculty's *Zones of Comfort, Risk and Danger* exercise (see Figure 5.1) that she adapted and revised (Wentworth, 2001).

To Ley (2011), discomfort is good. Risk is fine. But push-ing into the danger zone destroys trust and risks ending the coach's relationship with the teacher. She warns coaches against using body language, tone of voice, or questions that are too negative or judgmental; this can push conversations into the danger zone and cause teachers to shut down. Ley believes if Peer Coaches are careful to build and maintain a strong, trusting relationship, more challenging probing questions that emphasize student learning will encourage teachers to take bigger risks and adopt more innovative practices.

Each of these efforts to encourage risk taking suggest that friendly, constructive, supportive behavior is prerequisite to

Figure 5.1   Zones of Comfort, Risk, and Danger

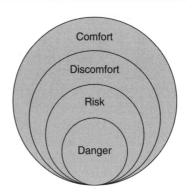

Source: Adapted by Ley from Wentworth (2001).

a coach's success, but creating a relationship based on trust and respect may not be enough to encourage innovation. Each of the strategies we just reviewed can serve to strengthen the coaching relationship by building the collaborating teacher's self-confidence. Self-confidence becomes another strand in the safety net. All of these strategies have another goal. They are designed to draw on the trust the coach has engendered so that the coach can push, nudge, and encourage his or her learning partner to move out of the comfort zone and take risks by adopting innovative teaching and learning strategies. These gentle nudges are critical to build the collaborating teacher's capacity to improve teaching and learning. Let's look at an example that gives us some insight into why this approach is so important.

Jennie Warmouth's introduction to Peer Coaching came from her collaboration with a coach who encouraged her to take a risk and try a project that Jennie had long wanted to attempt with students. This project excited students, it successfully achieved its learning goals, and it broadened Warmouth's goals. She believed her Peer Coach "provided me with a reciprocal and energizing relationship in which my ideas were welcome and problems were solved collaboratively," and she wanted to provide the same kind of support and innovative spark for others (J. Warmouth, personal communication, June 4, 2012). So she enrolled in Peer Coach training. Warmouth's first learning partners wanted assistance integrating technology into student learning. Warmouth was comfortable with this task, but there were some things that made her a little uneasy. She was young, and the two teachers she agreed to coach were much more experienced. She worried about the difference and was concerned about the fact that the teachers she was working with didn't want to make a mistake in front of their students. Warmouth felt she had to provide a lot of support to make these teachers comfortable. If she couldn't, she feared they would simply quit working with her. The teachers liked the idea that Warmouth would be "working behind the curtain" providing this high level of support (J. Warmouth, personal communication, June 4, 2012).

Working behind the curtain meant Warmouth listened to her peers talk about ways that technology could support their existing instruction. Warmouth used these discussions to shape very structured plans that had her providing hands-on tools and instruction. Warmouth took the lead in organizing agendas and typed up directions complete with screen shots. After some time, the collaborating teachers were using technology more often. But Warmouth began to worry if her "coaching style actually reinforced the very teacher-centered instructional dynamic that I was hoping they would transcend in their classrooms." Warmouth had hoped that in their third year together, she and her collaborating teachers would be ready to have "critical conversations about changing the nature of instruction," but she left the classroom for graduate school before she got the chance to have this conversation (J. Warmouth, personal communication, June 4, 2012).

Warmouth knew what she would do differently if she had it to do over. She told me she would be far less of a shepherd, do less of the work, and release a lot more responsibility for learning to her learning partners sooner, "even if they felt uncomfortable." And she would have "spent more time in their classrooms collaborating, working alongside of them, team-teaching, modeling, and assisting" (J. Warmouth, personal communication, June 4, 2012). Warmouth is not alone. Over the years, other Peer Coaches have described how they took on too much responsibility for learning and enabled learned dependence. Few have been as openly reflective about what was working, what wasn't, and what they would do differently.

Warmouth's experiences indicate that being friendly, positive, and supportive doesn't guarantee innovation, but coaches won't encourage innovation without drawing on these behaviors to create a safety net. Coaching success also requires that the learning

Being friendly, positive, and supportive doesn't guarantee innovation, but coaches won't encourage innovation without drawing on these behaviors to create a safety net.

partner take responsibility for her or his own learning. Her experiences also highlight the need for a coach to encourage a colleague to take risks.

Summary

Communication and collaboration skills are vital to help coaches build a relationship with peers, based on respect and trust, and assist peers to develop answers to the issues they face as they work to improve teaching and learning for their students. Effective coaches use these sets of skills and trust as a springboard to encourage their learning partners to take risks and adopt innovative teaching and learning practices.

- Communication skills, particularly probing questions, can play a vital role in encouraging teachers to think more deeply about their practice, take risks, and adopt innovative teaching practices.
- Communication and collaboration skills are learned behaviors and take constant practice and repetition in a variety of environments before educators are effective at using them.
- The coach and the collaborating teacher must agree on norms that ensure that the learner takes responsibility for the learning, and together they must continue to monitor their behavior to ensure that they remain individually and collective responsible for learning.
- Effective coaches use a variety of strategies to push, nudge, or encourage their learning partners to take risks to improve teaching and learning.

Defining Effective Learning Activities

Whole-system educational reform requires "a declared focus on concrete...describable innovative teaching practices."

—Michael Fullan (2011b)

One of the most serious challenges facing educators today is the disconnect between their belief that teaching and learning need to improve to meet their students' needs and a clear understanding of what kind of learning activities will help students develop these skills. One way that challenge presents itself to Peer Coaches every day is a result of our unprecedented access to information. In 2010, Eric Schmidt, the CEO of Google, told an audience that the amount of information being created every 2 days equals the amount of information created from the dawn of time until 2003 (Siegler, 2010). More than a decade before Schmidt's stunning statement, Sugata Mitra wondered what online access to information could mean for student learning. Mitra's novel experiments have shown that with the Internet and a need or interest, students can learn about anything without any help or guidance from a teacher (Judge, 2000). His research also raises serious questions for educators. What does easy student access to this tsunami of information mean for what and how they teach?

Proponents of 21st-century skills believe access to information means that there are at least two significant changes required. One change was clear to me when I happened on this headline on MSN: "Shirtless man repels raccoon with 'Hannah Montana' spray." We know students can find information, but this headline should cause us to question whether they can assess the validity of the information they find. Not so much, according to the Educational Testing Services (2006). If you need further evidence, look at student research papers, where you are likely to see students quoting the first website they find. Access to almost limitless amounts of completely unfiltered information means teachers don't need to emphasize teaching facts. Instead, they should offer learning activities that help students to develop the kind of information literacy needed to separate valid, valuable information from the chaff. Helping students become information literate is one small part of the challenge presented by the flood of new information.

The second, larger challenge educators face as a result of our unprecedented access to information is closely tied to the definition of the word *know*. Bransford, Brown, and Cocking (2000) concluded that online resources offer so much new information that "the meaning of 'knowing' has shifted from being able to remember and repeat information to being able to find and use it." They insist that learning needs to help students gather valid information, analyze and synthesize it, draw conclusions, and have the ability to transfer concepts and skills from one setting to another (p. 5). This kind of learning aligns perfectly with the type described by advocates of 21st-century learning.

Educators and the Peer Coaches that work with them find it easy to talk about 21st-century skills but much more difficult to turn abstract ideas like critical thinking, analyzing and synthesizing information, transference, information literacy, and creativity into practical classroom learning activities. Let me make this personal. As a history teacher, I accept the need for innovation, but I wonder what I need to do to move from teaching facts, names, and dates and asking students to repeat them. What are the characteristics of a learning activity that helps students develop the ability to analyze and synthesize information and draw conclusions? How do I get from names and dates to creativity? What content and instructional strategies do I need to use to help students develop these skills? How do I put these ideas into practice?

> Educators and the Peer Coaches that work with them find it easy to talk about 21st-century skills but much more difficult to turn abstract ideas like critical thinking, analyzing and synthesizing information, transference, information literacy, and creativity into practical classroom learning activities.

These are the very real questions that are stopping classroom innovation dead in its tracks. My experiences working with educators around the world suggest that many of them have not had meaningful discussions about how to turn these relatively vague ideas into practice. They don't have a clear, concrete understanding of the characteristics of a learning activity that will prepare students with these skills or the pedagogy required to offer students this kind of learning. Researchers have drawn the same conclusions. City and colleagues (2009) argue that teachers and administrators have specific expectations for student performance but are far less certain about what teachers need to do to reach these expectations, and they are unsure about how to do it. This is the very real world that Peer Coaches find themselves in on a daily basis. So how do you prepare Peer Coaches for this challenge?

- The first strategy is to help prospective Peer Coaches develop insight into the characteristics of learning that will prepare students with 21st-century skills.
- The second strategy uses these insights and research from the learning sciences to come to agreement on a norm for effective 21st-century learning. Let's explore the implementation of these strategies.

CHARACTERISTICS OF EFFECTIVE LEARNING

Collaboration, even highly effective collaboration, isn't enough to improve learning. Researchers in systemic educational reform have concluded that collaboration among teachers is critical, but it won't produce wide-scale improvement in teaching and learning unless all the educators in a school have explicitly agreed on concrete, describable teaching practices (Elmore, 2004; Fullan, 2011b). Both Elmore and Fullan maintain improving teaching and learning requires the educators in the school to explicitly agree on a norm for effective learning. Such a norm has long been part of Peer Coach training because it is essential to a coach's success.

> Collaboration, even highly effective collaboration, isn't enough to improve learning.

Think of what coaches do. They coplan learning activities, model a learning activity, or reflect after observation. All of these will founder unless there is an explicit agreement between the coach and the collaborating teacher on what *improvement* means. For evidence, let's look at the importance of such a norm for just one coaching role, providing feedback. In "The Art of Feedback", Armstrong (2012a) quoted a former principal who didn't convey what he would be evaluating before he provided feedback to teachers about their practice. When he offered feedback, he found "they might value it or they might not. Sometimes they would flatly disagree with what were best practices" (p. 1).

The norm for effective instruction is a road map that describes what teachers need to do to improve their practice and specifics on how to shape teaching and learning activities to reach their goals. How do Peer Coaches develop this norm for teaching and learning? Before Peer Coaches start to focus on the traits of effective learning, they have already discussed and defined what kinds of skills and competencies they believe that students need for success in their future. Peer Coach training draws on the conclusions of these discussions and prospective coaches' beliefs and experiences. These beliefs and experiences can be powerful tools for innovation. After more than two decades of working closely with educators, I have yet to find one who became a teacher to create a killer worksheet. They all dreamed of creating a learning activity that would actively engage students in gathering information, analyzing and synthesizing that information, and solving real problems. They believed that their students would be excited about the work they were doing because it had real meaning to them.

So how do you tap in to educators' beliefs and experiences to shape a norm for effective teaching and learning? One approach is to have prospective Peer Coaches review a video of a classroom learning activity that was shaped by the project-based learning model and has helped students develop some 21st-century skills. As they observe the video, prospective coaches identify the qualities of learning they are viewing. They often observe that students are actively involved in their learning. They might also note the students gathering, analyzing, and synthesizing information and drawing conclusions to solve real-world problems. They frequently point out the students' use of technology to collaborate or share their learning with a real-world audience (Meyer et al., 2011u).

Since the Peer Coaches' role is to encourage innovation, they may need fresh perspectives on innovative approaches to teaching and learning. Without this kind of outside stimulus, drawing on prior learning may only succeed in supporting the status quo. The discussion of the video offers such a perspective. Reading research about the four attributes of effective learning environments in *How People Learn* and studies on effective integration of technology give prospective coaches additional insights into alternatives to traditional approaches to teaching and learning.

If the educators involved in this activity were secondary school teachers, they would also review *Industrial Revolution Tic Tac Toe*, a project designed by a high school teacher in Indiana (Streeval, 2011, quoted in Meyer et al., 2011u). Autumne Streeval's ninth-grade students study the Industrial Revolution and use Tic Tac Toe (see Table 6.1) to compare the Industrial Revolution and modern industrialization to gain a better understanding of the global economy and social inequalities and an awareness of how industrialization relates to many aspects of society. As you review the activity, you will see it goes beyond a typical history project by asking students to integrate content from several content areas.

After prospective Peer Coaches review this learning activity, which includes the standards the project is designed to address, the students' tasks, directions, and the assessment process, they compare Tic Tac Toe with that they learned from the first learning activity they reviewed and the research on effective learning they read earlier.

Then the prospective coaches define the characteristics of effective learning, using the Chalk Talk protocol created by the National School Reform Faculty (Wentworth, n.d.). There is only one rule in this protocol: No talking. Participants discuss their ideas using chalk, markers, or computers. Since there are a lot of people communicating at the same time, the list of characteristics can be messy. To add some order, participants draw lines to link ideas that seem related. They can highlight those that seem really critical to them or use cartoon "text balloons" to raise questions about some point or add their thoughts on

Table 6.1   Industrial Revolution Tic Tac Toe

Directions: Select three project options to complete. You may select three across, three down, or three through the middle.

Photo Essay/Art	Research/Writing	Musical
Find pictures (or create your own) of working conditions during the Industrial Revolution age (1800s) and photos from our current time. Photos can show child labor, factories, housing, etc. Put them together in a collage using multimedia. Examples might be a PowerPoint, an online photo album on a site like Snapfish, a website, scrapbook, etc. Minimum of 20 pictures. Include captions with your pictures to provide a description of the images.	Research current child labor laws in the United States. Find out what the laws are and then consider: Should there be stiffer legislation? Should there be more careful monitoring of children's work by parents and teachers? What should the rules be regarding work hours and responsibilities? Should there be rules regarding interference with schoolwork? Punishments for violators? Write a letter to a policy maker or editor expressing your opinions based on your research.	Create a soundtrack of at least 10 songs that shows the working and living conditions during the Industrial Revolution and/or songs about working and living conditions today. Themes you might include are sickness, stress, low pay, pollution, etc. Design the cover of the CD as well as an explanation of why you selected those songs.
Drama	**Economics/Technical**	**Logical/Sequential**
Write and produce a movie based on the life of someone living during the Industrial Revolution. The person can be a member of the working poor, a wealthy capitalist, a middle-class individual, a child laborer, etc. You can act out the movie or use software to produce it.	Working conditions still vary widely depending on the work being performed and the area in which the work is located. Research global companies that have a good reputation for high-quality working conditions. Create a top 10 list of modern companies. Define your criteria and defend your list. Then create a recruitment advertisement for one of the companies. Ex: commercial, poster, website.	Create a series of charts that show rapid urban growth during the Industrial Revolution. Include information on population, productivity, average life span, pollution information, etc. Ex: Manchester and London (England), Lowell, Massachusetts.

(Continued)

Table 6.1   (Continued)

		Create the same series of charts that show rapid urban growth for modern times. Ex: China, India, etc.
Science/Health	**Technical**	**Creative Writing**
Poor and crowded living conditions during the Industrial Revolution led to the spread of many illnesses, including cholera. Research the causes, symptoms, and treatments for cholera. Then create a public service campaign to educate the masses about the illness. This can include posters, brochures, commercials, etc.	Many inventions were created during the Industrial Revolution. These include the seed drill, spinning jenny, cotton gin, steam engines, telephone, sewing machine, Morse Code (electrical signals over a telegraph), and railroad, among many others. Select three and create instructional/user manuals for the inventions. The manuals can be hand created or computer generated using software such as Publisher.	Imagine that you are living during the early years of the Industrial Revolution. Choose to be one of the following: a factory worker, a child laborer, or a working-class mother. Write a series of diary entries (at least five) in the role of your assumed character. Be sure to record the events of your day and include specific details about your life. You should include not only activities and observations but also your feelings and emotions.

Source: Streeval, n.d., quoted in Meyer et al., 2001u.

that idea (see Figure 6.1). By the time they have finished with this conversation, the participants have a fairly comprehensive list of the traits of highly effective learning (Meyer et al., 2011u). Each time I debrief this activity, participants say that they love the fact that all voices are heard in this silent conversation, not just those few that often dominate verbal discussions. Participants are keen to use this in staff meetings and

Figure 6.1   Chalk Talk Discussion

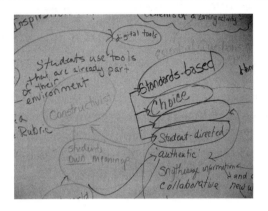

Source: Meyer et al. (2011u).

with students. Some use this tool as a quick formative assessment with their students. Try it in your classroom.

NORM FOR EFFECTIVE LEARNING

The key role professional development plays is to help teachers to evaluate learning activities by comparing them to their principles of effective learning.

—Grant Wiggins (L. Foltos, personal notes, October 2009)

Once the teams of prospective Peer Coaches have completed their definition of the traits of effective learning, it is important to ground their work in research and link their ideas and beliefs with what leaders in the field of learning are saying about the characteristics of effective learning. The team that created the curriculum for Peer Coaching was deeply influenced by the work of Eeva Reeder. Reeder was recognized by *Edutopia* and others for her work in project-based learning. She drew ideas from *How People Learn, Understanding by Design, Teaching for Understanding*, the Galileo Educational Network, and a number of other groups working on project-based learning to develop a comprehensive list of the characteristics of effective learning. She used this list in activities designed to encourage educators to think about the value of inquiry in learning activities. Reeder and the Peer Coaching team revised her synthesis and transformed it into the Learning Activity Checklist (see Table 6.2), a tool Peer Coaches and teachers can use to translate research into practice. Peer Coaches learn to use this checklist as they coplan learning activities with partners and as a critical tool for providing feedback to peers. It is Peer Coaches' norm for effective learning.

As you review the Learning Activity Checklist, you see there are four major characteristics of effective learning. These four characteristics are further defined by attributes that describe each of the four in more detail. It is important to note that an effective learning activity does not need to include every attribute for each of the characteristics of effective learning. For example, a project-based task need not ask students to form a reasoned judgment and solve a genuine problem and interpret a complex situation; it might be effective if it includes just one or two of these traits. But an effective learning activity needs to include at least some of the attributes from each of the four characteristics.

After reviewing and discussing the Learning Activity Checklist, prospective Peer Coaches compare it to the list of attributes they developed in the Chalk Talk activity, and they add attributes to the Learning Activity Checklist if they feel they add value. Then they discuss how to use this tool with the teachers they plan to collaborate with. This can be a serious issue for Peer Coaches.

Many prospective Peer Coaches have asked me, "What do I do if my peer asks me to improve a learning activity and I find none of the attributes from this checklist?" When I ask them what they might do, it is clear that they believe that sharing the checklist in these circumstances could overwhelm their colleagues and be wildly counterproductive.

> Many prospective Peer Coaches have asked me, "What do I do if my peer asks me to improve a learning activity and I find none of the attributes from this checklist?"

Table 6.2   Learning Activity Checklist

Standards-Based Task	Engaging Task
The task helps students: • Gain/improve specific knowledge or skills in a content area (state/national standards). • Gain/improve problem-solving, critical thinking, communication, collaboration, and other skills critical for college and careers. • Practice the methods/processes of a discipline (for example, the scientific method). • Understand the instructional goals for the learning activity. • Provide input on assessment standards. • Know and articulate the assessment procedures for activities. • Demonstrate understanding and apply their knowledge and skill in a variety of ways. • Reflect on, revise, and improve their work while engaged in learning. • Provide feedback on the learning activity and what they learned.	Students: • Are engaged in active learning (hands-on, making, moving, using multiple intelligences, etc.). • Find the topic fascinating, fun, passion arousing, and creativity encouraging. • Are given choices (topic, approach, etc.). • Are challenged (but not overwhelmed). • Bring their experiences outside the classroom to bear on their work. • Create a product/performance or gain competencies that have value to them and others outside of school. • Are engaged in peer learning, such as open discussion, and are accountable to one another. • Receive real-world feedback on their work from an audience or subject-matter expert from outside the school. • Apply what they learn to new, real-life problems or situations. • Create knowledge by drawing on what they have learned.
Problem-Based Task	**Technology Enhances Academic Achievement**
Students must exercise logical and creative thinking to: • Form a reasoned judgment. • Solve a genuine problem. • Make a decision or choice. • Plan a course of action. • Persuade or convince someone. • Interpret a complex situation.	Technology is used to: • Give students access to high-quality information, primary documents, or points of view not available otherwise. • Allow students to engage in learning activities that would otherwise be infeasible (for example, human/animal anatomy or online scientific investigations).

(Continued)

Table 6.2 (Continued)

• Resolve a perplexing or puzzling situation. • Troubleshoot and improve a system. • Apply a course concept in a real-world situation. • Invent a problem-solving process.	• Differentiate learning for students with different needs. • Help students understand abstract concepts. • Gather, organize, synthesize, and analyze information and draw conclusions. • Foster student discovery of a concept or construction of his or her own understanding of a concept. • Share ideas and collaborate with remote groups. • Help students receive feedback on their work from outside the classroom. • Enable students to participate in the democratic process.

Source: Reeder (2002, in Meyer et al., 2011n).

It might. In their conversations about how to use the Learning Activity Checklist, Peer Coaches insist this is not something that any coach would bring into a meeting with a peer, drop it on the table, and say, "Here it is; we are using this to guide our work. This is the model we are working toward."

Instead, coaches often tell me they might go through several steps before they introduce the Learning Activity Checklist. They may start by encouraging their peers to come up with a working definition of the skills and competencies their students need. Next, they may have a conversation with their peers about their school's educational goals and the kind of learning activities that support these goals. Many then ask their peers to define at least some attributes of learning essential to prepare students for their future. These coaches may use their peers' ideas to improve a learning activity without sharing the Learning Activity Checklist. Their reasons for doing that are based on terms that you have heard consistently: friendly, personalized, and manageable.

Many Peer Coaches believe that this approach is more likely to produce small but successful steps toward improvement that are critical to their long-term goal of improving teaching and learning. After these initial successes, these Peer Coaches finally introduce the Learning Activity Checklist, discuss it with their peers, and secure their peers' agreement that over time, they will work toward improving learning in ways consistent with the checklist. Once these conversations are behind them, the Peer Coaches can begin to use the Learning Activity Checklist as one tool that helps them collaborate with a peer to improve teaching and learning. Even at this point, it may be important for the Peer Coach to insist he or she won't be pushing to transform teaching and learning overnight. Instead, the coach and the learning partner may decide their short-term goals will emphasize incorporating ideas from only one characteristic from the checklist, like making a learning activity more engaging.

ASSESS LESSON DESIGN

Peer Coaches need a lot of practice using the Learning Activity Checklist as a tool to drive improvement in teaching and learning. Peer Coach training provides several classroom learning activities that teams of prospective Peer Coaches review and compare to each of the characteristics of effective learning defined in the Learning Activity Checklist. To give you a sense of what coaches do, I have included a brief description of a learning activity that prospective Peer Coaches assess (see Table 6.3). It doesn't have all the information, like standards, assessment plans, assessment tools, or project resources, that a Peer Coach might have. But there is enough information for you to use the Learning Activity Checklist to look for evidence of the ways the learning activity reflects each of the four main characteristics and ways that it might be improved. This activity isn't dangerous, so you can try this at home. If you are wondering how your assessment compares to that of others, look for those answers in Chapter 8.

Table 6.3   Study of Pollution in the Yamuna River

Grade 11 Chemistry, Language Arts

Nitin is a boy of 16 years who is staying near the banks of the Yamuna River, a tributary to the Holy River Ganga. Yamuna is also one of India's holiest rivers. He is using Yamuna water for drinking water, bathing, and irrigation. Recently he has had some skin disease, which the doctor says is because of the grossly polluted water of the Yamuna. This is not the only story from a resident staying near the Yamuna; there are similar diseases occurring to other people also.

As a responsible citizen leader, you need to identify the cause of the pollution problem in the Yamuna River and devise an action plan for mobilizing public opinion for checking the pollution. How can we solve this problem for our community?

Join a team of six students. Each team will:

- Identify the different types of water pollutants, their sources, and threats to human beings by conducting research online.
- Use public health websites and those of governmental environmental agencies.
- Participate in a lecture by a doctor on effects of water-borne disease.
- Discuss the types and different effects of water pollution.
- Visit the bank of the Yamuna and a nearby residential area.
  - o Interview senior citizens in the area to gather information about the state of the Yamuna in their memories.
  - o Use your discussions with senior citizens to make a chronology of the state of the Yamuna in different years.
  - o Explore the effects of industrialization in the area.
  - o Conduct a survey of water-borne diseases in the area.
  - o Collect water samples from different areas of the Yamuna and household drinking water.
  - o Take photographs.
- Get the pollution data from the Pollution Control Board for previous years.
- Visit the Pollution Control Office of Delhi and collect data pertaining to previous years in Yamuna.
- Test water samples in a chemistry lab.
- Analyze sources of pollution and Yamuna neighborhood health problems in the computer lab.
- Suggest ways to minimize the pollution from the major sources.
- Share your team's plan with the class. The best of the suggestions will be shared with the authorities, residents, and media to create a multiplier effect.
- Start an awareness campaign through a poster competition.

Source: Srivastava & Subrata (2007, quoted in Meyer et al., 2011a).

After prospective coaches have assessed a couple of learning activities using this process, a few things are apparent to them. They typically forget to use any of the communications skills they have been learning and practicing. These coaches will be the first to say they need a lot more practice assessing ways to strengthen a learning activity and use effective communications skills. Prospective coaches also recognize it is important to practice initially on learning activities created by someone they don't know, since they can be a bit judgmental and even pretty brutal in their feedback. I think it safe to say their first efforts wouldn't produce a trusting relationship. Practicing these skills on a learning activity created by someone the prospective coach knows comes a bit later, after they have had experience assessing and discussing several activities.

Start Positive

Successful coaches know that any discussion about how to improve a learning activity must begin with the coach describing what is good about the activity. "Good" means evidence of the ways that the learning activity supports each of the four characteristics in the Learning Activity Checklist. For example, coaches may describe evidence they found that it was a standards-based task as they reviewed the activity. Any coaching conversation about improving a colleague's work must start with a clear statement that praises what's good about the learning activity. The relationship between the coach and the learning partner may depend on this simple step. In any conversation that emphasizes what needs to be improved and how to improve it, egos will be on the line. The teacher whose work is being discussed can feel threatened. Starting with the positive gives teachers a sense of confidence and encourages their belief that they are building on something

> Any coaching conversation about improving a colleague's work must start with a clear statement that praises what's good about the learning activity.

that works and making it better. In their work on coaching, Bob and Megan Tschannen-Moran (2011) call this a strengths-based approach to coaching. Like many of the Peer Coaches I work with, these authors insist the starting point in any conversation about improving a learning activity needs to be what the teacher is currently doing well. Successful Peer Coaches move on to discuss what could be improved and ways to improve the learning activity only after they have identified the strengths in their learning partners' work.

Start Small

Prospective Peer Coaches also come to understand that when they begin working with a collaborating teacher, it will be critical to define just a few aspects of the learning activity the teacher wants to focus on improving. The reason is simple. I was working with a group of Swedish educators who assessed the Yamuna example (Table 6.3) and gave me suggestions for improvement in each of the four key characteristics found in the Learning Activity Checklist. Before they shared their thoughts, I asked them to assume I had created the learning activity and they were coaching me to improve it. I used this approach because it encouraged coaches to use those critical communication skills. These were very good teachers with years of experience using pedagogy like project-based learning, and they had a *lot* of suggestions for improvement. After about 30 minutes of nonstop suggestions, one of the educators observed, "You must be feeling pretty miserable because of all of the suggestions" (L. Foltos, personal notes, April 2009). I was. You could imagine what the teacher who created the activity would have felt like if he or she were in the room. I asked these educators what they would have done if a colleague brought this learning activity to them and asked them to help improve it.

Almost immediately, one of the group said **trying to assess the entire activity against all four characteristics in the Learning Activity Checklist was a recipe for disaster.**

Discussion of each of the four characteristics could produce so many possible areas for improvement that the teacher might not know where to start. Some of the participants noted that any effort to improve all four areas was likely to be overwhelming for a peer. Or worse, others suggested, the collaborating teacher might be more than overwhelmed; she or he might also be so depressed by the discussion as to not want to continue to collaborate with the coach (L. Foltos, personal notes, April 2009).

Several participants suggested **the coach needs to start small by asking the collaborating teacher what he or she wanted to emphasize before there was any serious discussion of how to improve the learning activity** (L. Foltos, personal notes, April 2009). Perhaps the teacher wants to make it more engaging for students by getting feedback on the students' work from others outside of the classroom. Or he or she may want help with formative assessment. Maybe this teacher wants to encourage more emphasis on critical thinking skills. The coach's job is to elicit from the teacher what the teacher wants to focus on, make sure that the scope of work outlined by the teacher is manageable, and focus the discussion of how to improve the activity only on those facets of lesson design important to that teacher.

Dozens of other groups of Peer Coaches have offered the same advice. This kind of all-encompassing assessment of a learning activity may work to help coaches develop the skills they need as they are being trained, but they insist it won't work in the school. The coach's job is to work with the teacher to define what he or she wanted to focus on and use the appropriate resources and tools to help meet that goal.

This approach can be a sure-fire method to bring the theory behind Peer Coaching to life. Coaching is an iterative process of continuous improvement. Starting small, with a carefully defined, teacher-driven focus, is one way to ensure the small successes that bring the teacher back to the coach with ideas for what to work on next. This approach to

Starting small, with a carefully defined, teacher-driven focus, is one way to ensure the small successes that bring the teacher back to the coach with ideas for what to work on next. This approach to coaching increases the odds that Peer Coaches can turn the theory of continuous improvement into practice.

coaching increases the odds that Peer Coaches can turn the theory of continuous improvement into practice.

After they have reviewed several learning activities and practiced this process of providing feedback, prospective coaches are ready to start to coach other participants in their training cadre. This time they are improving an activity created by people they know.

Summary

If the goal of coaching is to improve the quality of student learning activities, effective coaching requires that coaches and their learning partners explicitly agree on a norm for effective teaching and learning. This norm is essential to guide the work of the coaches and the teachers they collaborate with.

- Defining this norm requires educators to draw upon prior knowledge, experiences, and beliefs. It also requires thoughtful analysis of effective learning activities to identify other traits of effective teaching and learning.
- The norm also must be based on research in the field.
- Coaches need to learn to use this norm to assess learning activities. This can be a lengthy process that requires practice using the tool to assess a variety of learning activities. Ongoing feedback from those teachers they are collaborating with is an essential element of this process.
- Coaches become more effective at using communication skills by practicing them as an integral part of providing feedback aimed at improving learning activities.
- Once the coach and her or his collaborating teacher have agreed on a norm for effective learning, they apply this norm to the process of improving learning activities.

7

Lesson-Improvement Process

If we teach today as we taught yesterday, we rob our children of tomorrow!

—John Dewey

Learning activities, like those described in the last chapter, that encourage students to move from consuming information to creating knowledge as they solve real-world problems may not be part of the daily practice for many teachers. When teachers see examples of this kind of learning, it is clearly appealing to them. I know many who want their students to solve one of the challenges laid out in J. F. Rischard's (2002) book *High Noon: 20 Global Challenges, 20 Years to Solve Them* after hearing him describe them. Most often they have their students join established projects, like Deforest Action, which is one of the collaborative projects based on Rischard's

Many educators need both a research-based process for lesson design and resources related to that process as scaffolding to help them create similar learning activities. They are even more likely to adopt these innovative approaches to learning if they collaborate with a coach who can help them use the process and associated resources.

work. Educators can find Deforest Action and other high-quality learning activities their students can join on the Taking it Global website. Other teachers, like Pauline Roberts and Rick Joseph from Birmingham, Michigan, create their own learning activities that ask students to solve real problems. In their project, Doing Business in Birmingham, these two educators asked their fifth-grade students to work with local businesses to help those businesses become more environmentally friendly. The results were so powerful that local businesses began calling the classroom asking students what they could do to make the businesses greener. My experience suggests that some educators have the skills to create a similar project, but many educators need both a research-based process for lesson design and resources related to that process as scaffolding to help them create similar learning activities. They are even more likely to adopt these innovative approaches to learning if they collaborate with a coach who can help them use the process and associated resources.

The last chapter argued that preparing coaches to improve learning requires:

1. Helping prospective Peer Coaches develop insight into the characteristics of learning that will prepare students with 21st-century skills.

2. Using these insights and research from the learning sciences to come to agreement on a norm for effective 21st-century learning.

These two are just half the skills effective Peer Coaches need to assist peers in improving learning activities. In this chapter, we will learn more about two closely related skills, including how Peer Coaches:

3. Learn to use a lesson-design process and related resources that support the process of improving teaching and learning.

4. Gain experience using the communication skills essential to coplan learning activities and provide feedback to others.

Peer Coach training provides a relatively simple lesson-design process, related resources, and time for the coaches to learn about and use these tools. In their training, Peer Coaches work to improve a learning activity that is commonly used in their school, like a fifth-grade state report or a research project on an author, a book, or a historical figure. In other words, coaches learn about lesson design while working on an activity that is relevant to them. Peer Coaches collaborate with another coach to improve this lesson, a tactic that gives these partners experience using the process and the resources for lesson improvement that they will use with colleagues at their school, and practice collaborating with peers to improve learning activities.

While coaches often look for a partner for this activity who teaches at their grade level or teaches the same subject, some of the most effective collaborations have been between educators who teach at different grade levels or in different subject areas. One of the strongest collaborative projects I have seen was created by teachers who taught high school physics and third grade. When you ask these unlikely duos what contributed to their successes, they insist that both partners were viewing the problems with fresh eyes, because they are viewing the issue from vastly different perspectives. They also talk about the fact that they feel like they can be more creative when they are working in an area that is beyond their comfort level. Some successful Peer Coaches like this model so well they brought it back to their schools. As I noted in Chapter 3, at one high school near Sydney, Australia, all six coaches at the school work with teachers who teach a different subject. The school took this approach because it wanted to encourage differing perspectives and cross-curricular learning (J. Linklater, personal communication, June 14, 2012).

CREATE A TASK

One of the first things Peer Coaching facilitators ask the teams of coaches to do is to create a task for the students. For many teachers who teach from the textbook and emphasize didactic learning, a task is a new concept. Tasks are essential in learning that asks students to play an active role in solving real-world problems and develop 21st-century skills. They hook the students, engage their interest in a learning activity, and define how students will demonstrate their learning. So what shapes a good task? I think we all understand that if the problems come from the real world, they will be complex, not easy to solve, and that there probably is more than one good answer. Bransford, Brown, and Cocking (2000) remind educators that real-world problems have to have meaning to their students in their community and need to draw on students' current knowledge, skills, beliefs, and passions.

How do coaches translate these somewhat abstract ideas into a task that makes sense for students? First, they need to understand that tasks often consist of two elements: a scenario that will stimulate students' interest, give them an understandable setting, and define an audience along with an essential question that is designed to define the product the students will create (Meyer et al., 2011j). In a strong task, that product helps students make sense of important, complicated ideas and also helps students to develop critical thinking and problem-solving skills (Coalition of Essential Schools, n.d.; Wiggins, 2007). To help coaches understand this, Peer Coach training has them review tasks, like the "before" and "after" tasks in the example found in Table 7.1, to see how these ideas are put into practice. This is one of those experiments you *can* try at home. How do the revisions make this task more engaging and authentic?

Earlier I noted that the lesson-improvement process consisted of both a process for lesson design and supporting resources. We have explored a bit of the process educators might use to write an effective task. To ensure that Peer Coaches and their learning partners have the knowledge essential to write a strong task, every coach uses the Learning Activity Checklist, particularly those sections that deal with problem-based and engaging tasks, as they write their task. To encourage deeper thinking about essential questions, prospective coaches read and discuss Grant Wiggins's (2007) article "What Is an Essential Question?" This discussion stresses the value of using essential questions and the qualities of a good essential question. If Peer Coaches feel they need more information on essential questions, they might use the Galileo Educational Network's article on creating essential questions (Clifford & Friesen, 2007). Once the teams have developed a task, they include it in the template for learning activities found in Table 7.2.

Table 7.1   Task Comparison

Task Before	Task After
Your teacher recently talked about being aware of the number of grams of fat, sodium, and calories in your diet and why it is important to know this information. You will calculate the nutritional value of what you eat at a fast food restaurant.	You are in a hurry to get to practice and decide to catch a bite to eat on your way. Your teacher recently talked about being aware of the number of grams of fat, sodium, and calories in your diet and why it is important to know this information. And your coach has been talking about how nutrition can make a difference in how well your team plays. How healthy is your favorite fast food meal? What can you learn that could help you and your teammates choose fast food that is both tasty and healthy?

Source: Meyer et al. (2011j).

Table 7.2   Lesson Improvement Template: Task

Lesson Title:	
Grade Level(s):	
Content Area(s):	
Student Task: What real problem situation will students address? What useful product(s), event(s), or service(s) will students produce? What audience might benefit from the students' work?	

Source: Meyer et al. (2011q).

DEFINE STANDARDS

There are three groups of standards educators should include in their learning activities: curriculum standards, 21st-century standards, and technology standards (Meyer et al., 2011m). Curriculum standards define what students at various grade levels should know about specific subjects and how they could demonstrate that learning. In the United States, most educators use standards drawn from the Common Core State Standards. I urge Peer Coaches to restrain the natural impulse to include every standard that might be related to the project. Two or three of these content standards are enough if educators are asking students to work on short-duration projects. In these kinds of activities, there won't be enough time for students to develop skills in more than a few areas. Nor will the educators who assign the work be able to assess the students' mastery of a large number of standards.

Peer Coaching training also asks educators to include 21st-century skills. The Common Core State Standards include more emphasis on 21st-century skills than many of the standards created by individual states, but Peer Coaches and their learning partners should decide if the standards they are working toward place enough emphasis on 21st-century skills. If they feel there is a need to include a specific 21st-century skill, like those defined by Partnership for 21st Century Skills, I suggest they include no more than one (Partnership for 21st Century Skills, n.d.). Finally, many curricular standards do not emphasize the integration of technology, so educators may want to include a relevant standard drawn from the student technology standards, known as NETS•S, which were created by the International Society for Technology in Education (ISTE, 2007; Meyer et al., 2011m). Once the team members have defined their standards, they add them to their template; see Table 7.3.

LEARNING CONTEXT

As we have seen throughout this book, innovative learning places a strong emphasis on helping students to develop 21st-century skills and use and apply them in a variety of settings. Since the development of these skills often means teachers need to help students develop them over time and in a variety of educational activities, the context of the learning activity the coach and teacher are improving becomes critical.

In a traditional classroom, context was simple to determine. Teachers covered the material in the textbook. Determining the context was as simple as looking at what students learned in the preceding chapter and what they would learn in the subsequent chapter (Meyer et al., 2011o). Many educators argue this approach encourages learning that is a mile wide and an inch deep. The authors of *How People Learn* (Bransford et al., 2000) offer a new meaning for the term *context*. Instead of superficial coverage, Bransford and colleagues (2000) insist, "Teachers must teach some subject matter in depth, providing many examples in which the same concept is at work and providing a firm foundation of factual knowledge" (p. 20). Helping students develop these more complex skills may require a series of carefully sequenced learning activities. Context in this environment is critical.

Peer Coaches and their peers define how the learning activity they are improving relates to their overall plans to help students master the chosen standards, particularly those that focus on higher-order skills like critical thinking or problem solving. To guide their process, prospective coaches address the three questions raised in Table 7.3, the Lesson Improvement Template.

Table 7.3   Lesson Improvement Template: Context, Standards, and Assessment

Learning Context: What is the context in which this lesson occurs in your curriculum?	• What prerequisite knowledge or understanding is necessary for learning? • How does the learning activity relate to previous learning and in particular to other activities that will help students develop the same types of skill and knowledge? • How will students be able to explain what they are doing, why they are doing it, and how the activity relates to previous learning activities?
Assessment Plan and Resources	
What standards or learning objectives will be addressed in students' products and performances?	**Outline your assessment plan here.** When and how will you provide feedback during the lesson? How will student progress be measured toward the selected standards? Include relevant elements of your assessment plan in the student directions. Create and attach assessment tools or describe your feedback strategies here.
<Insert Standards>	Assessment plan Examples of assessment tools Feedback strategies

Source: Meyer et al. (2011q).

STUDENT DIRECTIONS

The directions that teachers provide to students are the next step of the lesson-improvement process. These directions need to offer students a road map to solve the task their teacher outlined. As teachers shape these directions, Peer Coaching training strongly encourages that the directions include one trait from the Learning Activity Checklist: They should give students choices in what and how they learn. Second, the directions should draw on the ideas of Bransford and colleagues (2000) and encourage students to collaborate in ways that develop a classroom community of learners who help each other learn (Meyer et al., 2011x).

Helping teachers define what students should do to solve the task may require scaffolding. For Peer Coaches and their peers, the Peer Coaching training offers a variety of resources to provide the necessary support, including access to a variety of promising practices websites that include reviewed learning activities. Coaches and learning partners might explore Thinkfinity, CIESE Online Classroom Projects, and the WebQuest Page. Other resources introduce the Big 6 and other information-literacy resources for finding, organizing, assessing, and using information well. In addition, resource materials bring educators to a number of scaffolding tools designed to help students organize and use information needed to address challenging, perhaps complex tasks (Meyer et al., 2011x).

The last step in this process of creating directions for students asks educators to check that they have aligned these directions with the standards they hope students will master. Often I find that the standards the teacher hope students will master emphasize critical thinking, problem solving, and creativity. For example, the teacher may expect students to reach a standard related to critical thinking by explaining whether the Founding Fathers would vote for Tea Party candidates in 2012. But the directions ask students to gather and record factual information about two of the Founding Fathers and two of the Tea Party's key ideas. Clearly there is a disconnect between the standards and the directions in this learning activity. To help bridge the potential gap between directions and standards, educators need to review both and then answer two questions: What skills, particularly 21st-century skills, do you want students to develop? If students follow your directions, will they develop these skills?

> To help bridge the potential gap between directions and standards, educators need to review both and then answer two questions: What skills, particularly 21st-century skills, do you want students to develop? If students follow your directions, will they develop these skills? (Meyer et al., 2011x)

(Meyer et al., 2011x). If the creator of the Founding Fathers activity had answered these questions, the teacher would have had to revise the directions he or she described for students so that the students were gathering a different type of information and then analyzing that information to draw conclusions.

Once the teams are confident they have supplied the necessary directions and their directions are consistent with their standards, they add these directions to the template (see Table 7.4). At this point, they will also include any directions students might need to integrate technology, a topic we will explore in more detail in the next chapter. Their facilitators also encourage them to add any tips or directions another teacher might need to adapt and adopt the activity, since the improved lessons are shared with others in the Peer Coaching community.

REFLECTION AND FEEDBACK

As they complete the lesson-improvement process, it is also important for Peer Coaches to return to their role as coaches periodically. All of their previous experience providing advice on how to improve learning activities came from offering feedback on lessons created by anonymous sources. Coaches

Table 7.4   Lesson Improvement Template: Procedure

What directions and resources do students need to complete the lesson? What directions must teachers follow? (These teacher directions may also be tips for other teachers who want to adapt your activity.) How will technology enhance learning for students or teachers?		
Student Directions	**Teacher Tips**	**Technology to Be Used (What and How)**
<Insert Student Directions>	<Insert Directions/Tips>	<Insert Technology into Student Directions>

Source: Meyer et al. (2011q).

also need experience assessing and improving learning activities created by someone they know, which requires coaches to be more diligent about using the communication skills they learned earlier. So each team working on improving a learning activity pairs up with another team. Each team member presents a portion of the learning activity he or she has been improving, and each member of the other team assumes the role of coach and provides feedback. Then the teams switch roles. After each coach has given and received feedback, they all share what they found valuable and effective about the kind of feedback they received, a practice that helps coaches make feedback more effective. As they practice using their communication skills to offer feedback, Peer Coaches also find it is critical to rely on their norm for effective learning, the Learning Activity Checklist, to guide and shape the feedback they provide (Meyer et al., 2011v).

ASSESSMENT

The next step in the lesson-improvement process is developing an assessment plan and the tools essential to implement that plan. Many teachers are skilled at summative assessment, which provides students with information on the strengths and weaknesses of a project after they have completed their work. Bransford and colleagues (2000) insist that in addition to the end-of-activity assessments, educators must use formative assessment, which gives learners opportunities to receive feedback at benchmarks

> Educators must use formative assessment, which gives learners opportunities to receive feedback at benchmarks along the way, "to revise and improve the quality of their learning...while they are engaged in learning new materials" (Bransford, et al., 2000, pp. 24–25).

along the way, "to revise and improve the quality of their learning . . . while they are engaged in learning new materials" (pp. 24–25). In the world outside of school, this is the way most of us learn.

Students aren't the only ones who can benefit from using formative assessments. Teachers can also learn and improve while their students are working on a learning activity. Rather than waiting until the conclusion of an activity to reflect on what worked and what they would do differently next time, educators who use formative assessment throughout the learning process can make crucial midcourse adjustments to teaching and learning.

The lesson-improvement process used by Peer Coaches asks educators to develop an assessment plan that includes ongoing formative assessments as well as summative assessment (Meyer et al., 2011b). In addition, they develop rubrics, checklists, and other assessments needed to measure student progress toward meeting the standards (see Table 7.3). For those educators who need additional information on formative assessment, refer to articles by Judith Dodge ("What Are Formative Assessments and Why Should We Use Them?" 2009), Stephan Chappuis and Jan Chappuis ("The Best Value in Formative Assessment," 2007/2008), and Roberta Furger ("Take a Deeper Look at Assessment for Understanding," 2002). Each of these offers the kind of information and resources educators need to understand and implement effective formative assessments (Meyer et al., 2011b).

Another valuable resource is the section of the Learning Activity Checklist that focuses on standards-based tasks. It encourages educators to ensure that students understand the instructional goals for the learning activity, that they know and can articulate the assessment procedures for activities and to give students opportunities to provide input on the assessment standards (Meyer et al., 2011n). Many teachers routinely share assessment procedures with students before the students begin working on an activity, but it is less common that they solicit student input on the assessment standards. If they aren't using any of these approaches to assessment, their coaches can help them to adopt one or more. The Learning Activity Checklist also encourages teachers to have the students provide feedback on the learning activity and what they learned. For many teachers, the idea that they give students a role in assessing their own work could be new. This might be an area that teachers decide they want to emphasize in their work with a coach.

Over the years, I have seen many assessment strategies with one common weakness: They measure student activity by asking questions like the following: Did the students write a strong introductory paragraph? Do the students provide adequate and convincing resources to support their thinking and arguments? How well written is the students' work? If students are producing a video, the assessment may evaluate how well the images or sound the students include supports their arguments. Sometimes the sum of all these questions may measure whether the students reached the standard the activity was designed to meet. Often they don't, and assessment of progress toward reaching the standard is missing. So as the last step of the lesson-improvement process, educators review their assessment strategy and tools to ensure that the assessment really measures student progress toward reaching each standard included in the learning activity (Meyer et al., 2011b). Once the educators have completed their assessment strategies and tools, they add them to their lesson-improvement template (see Table 7.3).

RESOURCES

The last two elements that educators add to their improved lessons are the resources they want students to use and the sources of information (see Table 7.5) they have included to guide their students' work.

By the time a Peer Coach has completed this lesson-improvement process, her or his learning activities are invariably greatly improved, as are the coach's abilities to use communication skills to coach another teacher through the process of improving a learning activity. This highly collaborative lesson-improvement process also offers Peer Coaches deep insights into the value of coplanning learning activities and, in a broader sense, the value of collaboration. Since the activity focuses on giving and receiving feedback, it is a powerful opportunity for coaches to practice and sharpen their

Table 7.5   Lesson Improvement Process: Resources

What materials and other resources are needed for this lesson? List the curriculum, technology, and information resources the teacher and students will use to complete the lesson, including links to tutorials for software or process guides.		
Curriculum:	Technology:	Information Sources:

Source: Meyer et al. (2011q).

communication skills as they work collaboratively with a peer to improve a learning activity—the heart of a coach's work.

Summary

If the goal of coaching is to improve the quality of student learning activities, effective coaching requires coaches to apply their communications skills with lesson-design processes and resources that will guide their work with collaborating teachers.

- Most coaches and teachers benefit from using a process and resources to scaffold their efforts at designing and improving learning activities.
- Coaches and collaborating teachers need to use the norm for effective learning they defined earlier throughout the process of improving learning activities.
- Coaches need practice and experience using the lesson-improvement process and resources before they are ready to assist another teacher to improve a learning activity.
- Learning to use their communications skills in the context of providing feedback aimed at improving another teacher's learning activities is critical.

8

Enhancing Learning by Integrating Technology

Technology is not like fire, it aids learning through pedagogy and content.

—Chris Dede, (L. Foltos, personal notes, June, 2008)

If teachers ask students to solve problems that have meaning to them and others outside of school, there is a strong likelihood students will be communicating, collaborating, gathering and analyzing information, and expressing their learning in creative ways. Most likely, students will be using hardware and software. When it comes to integrating technology into classroom learning, part of the teachers' dilemma is deciding what technology to include. The blackboard has the same half-life as plutonium. Technology seems to have the same shelf life as milk and produce. It almost needs a

> Peer Coaches can assist teachers to choose by helping them to define the tasks, like communication or collaborating, they want students to perform. Experienced coaches use this as the starting point to assist teachers to identify and use the hardware and software that might best meet those requirements.

"Best if used by" date on it. New, often more effective technology is created so quickly that teachers don't feel like they can keep up with the onslaught. Peer Coaches can assist teachers to choose by helping them to define the tasks, like communication or collaborating, they want students to perform. Experienced coaches use this as the starting point to assist teachers to identify and use the hardware and software that might best meet those requirements.

In his witty article *Closing the Digital Divide: 7 Things Education and Educators Need to Do,* Ian Jukes (2008) insists that teachers need "techno fluency." What is techno fluency? It is an understanding of technology and how it might help a teacher reach his or her goals. So we might say it is technological literacy for educators. Jukes suggests educators develop this form of fluency by going on his "digital diet." This diet consists of trying some new technology each week for 25 weeks. Jukes argues the educators' diet should include using social networking sites like Facebook, using messaging software, reading and creating blogs, downloading and listening to podcasts, finding a relevant video on YouTube, or reading a Wikipedia article that has meaning to the teacher.

Like any diet, this one is destined to be altered, and Peer Coaches often revise it. They work on the premise that people are more successful when they diet together. So their first change is to make the diet highly collaborative. The coach and peer might explore "best practice" sites together and look for learning activities with learning goals similar to the one the teacher wants to improve. Working as a team, they can discuss what they might learn and use from these activities. They can also explore what technology the best-practice activity used to reach specific goals. If the tools in the best-practice site don't seem appropriate or effective to the teacher, the coach may look for some similar, perhaps newer technology to support the specific goals of the learning activity they are improving. Many Peer Coaches encourage their learning partners to invite their students to join this conversation about choosing technology.

Peer Coaches may want to broaden the collaborative circle in the search for answers because students can be incredible resources. Many have much more experience using technology than educators do and can play a role in defining what technology to use in a project. They can also help other students to use unfamiliar tools in classroom learning. Since we are all learners, it's important that we model this by learning from students. Don't ignore their potential. Effective coaches often extend the search for answers beyond the school; the world is full of teachers struggling with the same issues. Many coaches encourage their peers to explore Twitter groups, blogs, or online forums that tap into local or global learning communities to gain insights into the issues they are addressing, like choosing technology.

The idea of trying 25 technologies in 25 weeks may make teachers techno-fluent and help them think about how technology can help them reach their goals. For at least some teachers, their ability to apply what they learned may be a product of the diet, but for others, the diet could produce just-in-case professional learning. In this case, the teachers are learning about new tools just in case they find a use for them in their classrooms at some point in the future. So coaches alter the diet to seek a purposeful and immediate link between the learning goals in a specific learning activity and the new technology the teacher learns about.

Coaching: Linking Learning and Technology

The idea of focusing on powerful pedagogy to define how technology can enhance learning is a strategy that educators and organizations that promote the effective use of technology have long advocated. ISTE's (2007) national educational technology standards for students, known as NETS•S, begin by identifying educational tasks like communication, collaboration, critical thinking, or problem solving and then encourage teachers to identify and use appropriate digital resources to reach these learning goals. As clear and straightforward as this idea is, for many teachers, it hasn't proven easy to put into practice. Too often, teachers still plan their lessons around technology instead of putting learning first. What these teachers need to make the connection is a collaborative partner, a coach, who will help them focus first on learning and then choose the technology that will help students reach the learning goals.

Peer Coach training encourages coaches to work with their learning partners to explore the learning activity they are improving and look for tasks that ask students to communicate, collaborate, gather information, organize information, and encourage creative expression (Meyer et al., 2011p). This is the first step in the process of integrating technology. Together, the coach and learning partner have defined clear educational needs, and they are ready to determine if technology can enhance learning by meeting these needs. If the answer is yes, the teacher, the students, and the coach can learn just enough about the technology they want to use just in time to use it in the project. Some of the questions a coach might ask the teacher about how technology can support learning include the following:

- **Communication**—Does the learning activity encourage students to communicate with other students to gather information or complete the learning activity? Are the students communicating with others in their community to brainstorm about problems they are solving? Are they communicating to get feedback from real-world subject matter experts?
- **Collaboration**—Does the task ask students to collaborate with others in their local or global community to solve real-world problems or get feedback on their proposed solutions?
- **Gathering information**—To complete the learning task, do students need to gather information to draw

conclusions and create knowledge? While they are shaping their thinking and drawing conclusions, does the task require students to get feedback from subject matter experts outside the school? Does the assessment strategy require students to gather feedback while they are working on a project, information that might help improve their learning?

- **Organizing information**—Is the task shaped in ways that require students to organize, analyze, and synthesize information they have gathered?
- **Expression**—Are students demonstrating their learning by sharing their solutions to real-world problems? Are they sharing their learning with the community outside the school? Does the task encourage students to present their work in creative ways that are meaningful to them? Is the ability to include images, video, music, or dialogue important to expression?

Coaches who assist teachers in identifying software or hardware that helps students complete learning tasks are playing a key coaching role. The ISTE (2011) standards for coaches, NETS•C, call for coaches to assist teachers in selecting and using technology for student research, collaboration, and developing creativity and higher-order thinking skills. Let's explore what this standard might mean in the classroom. The second-grade teacher who wants to encourage her students to use images, video, sounds, and narration to demonstrate their learning may need assistance identifying relevant software. For example, the teacher may want the coach's help finding software that encourages her students to spend their time expressing their ideas clearly, not learning and manipulating complex video editing software. The teacher may also need help learning to use the tool. The coach might suggest this teacher turn to her students, but it is possible that the coach will provide some training. At this point, coaches face the same dilemma as teachers. Technology changes so quickly that a coach can't possibly know how to use all of the available software. Coaches don't need to; they just need to know where to find tutorials that they and their peers can use. Internet4classrooms.com, Microsoft, Google, and Apple's tutorials for educators are great starting places for commonly used software.

This strategy of identifying common tasks in the learning activity focuses on the core of teaching: How will the students learn and demonstrate what they have learned? When coaches ask if the task requires students to gather information, collaborate with others, present their findings, and get feedback, they are asking teachers to work in a realm they know and understand. With teaching and learning as starting points, coaches can emphasize how a specific piece of technology might help students to reach the goals and perform the tasks that the teacher has defined. Coaches who play this role help us meet another valuable—and largely unmet—need, encouraging teachers to use technology routinely.

> When coaches ask if the task requires students to gather information, collaborate with others, present their findings, and get feedback, they are asking teachers to work in a realm they know and understand.

As technology was introduced into classrooms more than 25 years ago, many leaders held the belief that it had the power to transform learning. Technology held a power that many leaders and prophets said couldn't be denied. I remember listening to nationally recognized leaders in the early 1990s telling us that technology was like a steamroller headed down the street, aimed right at educators. Educators had two choices: jump on the steamroller or become part of the pavement. Apparently, they overlooked a third option: Educators could step aside. And they did. The most recent broad assessment of teachers' use of information and communication technologies (ICT) was done by the National Education Association and the American Federation of Teachers. It concluded that all American educators have some access to computers and the Internet; about half felt adequately prepared to integrate technology into instruction. Only a third asked students to use technology in problem solving and research a few times a week (National Education Association, 2008, pp. 17–18). So for all practical purposes, two-thirds stepped aside. Here is a test you can try to see if the situation has changed. The next time you visit a school, ask anyone you meet who is doing a great job of using technology to support 21st-century learning. You can always find a handful of teachers, but typically there are only a few islands of excellence.

How can coaches assist and encourage more teachers to use these learning tools in more effective learning activities? The answer may relate to some of the strategies we have already discussed, but it also requires that coaches and the teachers they work with rethink the purposes for integrating technology.

TEST SCORES AND TECHNOLOGY INTEGRATION

"In Classroom of Future, Stagnant Scores" is the headline of a *New York Times* article about Kyrene School District, an Arizona district that had invested heavily in classroom technology. Classrooms were equipped with laptops, big interactive screens, and software for every basic subject. The result, the article concluded, was that "hope and enthusiasm are soaring here. But not test scores. Since 2005, scores in reading in math have stagnated in Kyrene, even as statewide scores have risen" (Richtel, 2011). Why, you're probably asking, would a chapter about integrating technology discuss this article? Before we can talk about how coaches help teachers integrate technology, it is important that we define the purpose for technology integration.

This article defines integration in terms of raising student scores on a standardized test that places very little emphasis on 21st-century learning. Like the

> More than 25 years after the introduction of technology into classrooms, American schools are still aiming for the lowest common denominator, using technology to increase standardized test scores.

high-stakes tests students in many states take each year, this test focuses on the basics. This article didn't invent this definition of technology integration. It simply reflects the reality in American schools. More than 25 years after the introduction of technology into classrooms, American schools are still aiming for the lowest common denominator, using technology to increase standardized test scores.

Many of those interviewed for this *New York Times* article insisted that emphasizing the use of technology to improve student test scores didn't adequately measure the value of technology in classrooms. Karen Cator, the educational technology lead in the U.S. Department of Education, maintained that "test scores are the same, but look at the other things students are doing: learning to use the Internet to research, learning to organize their work, learning to use professional writing tools, learning to collaborate with others" (quoted in Richtel, 2011). Measuring the impact of technology on standardized tests, Cator and others featured in the article insisted, didn't capture the breadth of skills that technology can help students to develop.

Almost in the same breath, those who extolled the virtues of technology admitted that standardized tests are currently the best way to "gauge the educational value of expensive technology investments" (Richtel, 2011). What a conundrum. Educators believe ICT can be powerful learning tools, but they can't currently measure their impact. So our "best" assessment system links test scores and ICT, which encourages teachers to use technology to support traditional instruction. We do need to recognize that testing isn't the only factor here. School leaders have done little to challenge this definition or provide most teachers with the support they need to adopt a different instructional model.

In an ideal world, new assessment tools that measure the impact of technology on 21st-century learning would be in the hands of educators today. There are some things that can't wait for a new assessment tool. Educational leaders need to redefine what it means to integrate technology in a way similar to Cator's efforts with the *New York Times*. And these leaders need to do it now. This same *New York Times* article noted that a 1997 presidential commission recommended the nation's schools should press ahead with deployment of technology while researchers determined the impact of technology in the classroom. Since that commission issued its report, an entire generation of children has entered and graduated from our schools. A second generation is now in enrolled. Educators are no closer to having research on the impact of technology or assessments to measure that impact than they were in 1997. Educators need to adopt a new definition of "integrating technology" now so that they can immediately begin to develop the skills needed to act on that definition.

It's Not About the Technology, It's About the Learning

Some years ago, Chris Dede observed, "Technology is not like fire, it aids learning through pedagogy and content" (L. Foltos, personal notes, June 2008). Many of us would agree that if you add fire to raw food, it improves the taste, but we would wonder how this metaphor helps educators understand what it means to integrate technology into teaching and learning effectively. The metaphor tells us that technology integration:

- Is not something separate from content and pedagogy
- Will not transform traditional teaching and learning
- Requires a clear focus on instructional goals and strategies used to reach those goals
- Is effective when it supports and enhances 21st-century pedagogy and content

Let's explore some common strategies for technology integration that demonstrate the value of applying Dede's perspective.

Technology as Play-Doh

Since the first computers came into classrooms, there have been some teachers who viewed technology as something separate from the curriculum. I have often heard teachers tell their classes, "This morning you are going to the computer lab." When you talked to students about their visit to the computer lab, it was clear that they saw no relationship between classroom learning and computers. Moving computers into classrooms didn't change this view of technology for every teacher. As Tracy Watanabe puts it, for some teachers, classroom use of technology "was like using Play-Doh in the classroom, it was separate from the curriculum" (T. Watanabe, personal communication, July 8, 2011). For at least some teachers, the idea that technology is divorced from their curriculum lives on.

Transforming Traditional Teaching and Learning?

> "I was convinced," she wrote, "that by helping teachers integrate technology into their lessons (doing the same thing...just with technology) would make the difference." (Sylvia Tolisano, 2009)

Sylvia Tolisano offered a crystal-clear explanation of a more prevalent approach to using ICT. "I was convinced," she wrote, "that by helping teachers integrate technology into their lessons (doing the same thing...just with technology) would make the difference" (Tolisano, 2009). Educators who embrace this view of technology integration hope that technology will transform teaching and learning even if teachers continue to teach the same textbook content and employ traditional teacher-centered pedagogy. Tolisano's definition of the term *technology integration* is one that has many adherents in classrooms today.

Much to the chagrin of those who believe technology could transform education, Dede's fire metaphor has no meaning when educators use technology to support traditional classroom learning. Almost anyone hoping to see the use of technology transform the learning process expected to see something significant as teachers began to

> Adding technology hasn't changed traditional teaching and learning, but it has made poor pedagogy more expensive.

use technology. Instead, close observation reveals that traditional activities that integrate technology still focus on finding, recording, and repeating facts, but students use technology to perform those tasks. Students may be submitting essays or reports using technology; too often, in these reports they are simply retelling or repeating factual information they gathered from books or online resources. Far from transforming learning, technology simply supports traditional instruction. What happens when you add ICT to traditional didactic instruction? In a large-scale study of the impact of technology use in fourth- and eighth-grade classrooms, Harold Wenglinsky (1998) found that focusing fourth- and eighth-grade students' use of technology on skill and drill exercises in math on computers was, in essence, worse than doing nothing. Adding technology hasn't changed traditional teaching and learning, but it has made poor pedagogy more expensive.

Dede's observation about the interrelationship of technology, pedagogy, and content does give educators a powerful lens to use in their efforts to rethink the use of technology. In her comments to the *New York Times* reporter (Richtel, 2011), Karen Cator insisted that technology was being used to support learning tasks that were often different from those in traditional classrooms. At least some of the tasks she identified would be found in the upper reaches of Bloom's Taxonomy, and some are 21st-century skills. ISTE's (2007) NETS•S technology standards make the interrelationship of technology and 21st-century pedagogy even more explicit. The standards are all aimed at integrating technology to help students develop critical thinking, collaboration, communication, and problem-solving skills, as well as developing creativity and innovation. These are the kinds of skills that we need to use to redefine what it means to integrate technology. Let's explore an example of the kind of learning Cator, ISTE, and others want teachers to adopt to help us frame a new definition.

Supporting and Enhancing 21st-Century Learning

Several years ago, a few students came to class in their school in southern England and wanted to talk about a

TV news report that explored the impact of raising poul-
try in factory-like conditions. These students suggested
that the class explore whether free-range or battery-raised
farming—producing birds on an industrial scale in factory-
like settings—was better for the chickens and those who con-
sumed them. The rest of the students agreed. Dan Roberts, the
teacher of this high school biology class, understood how the
topic could help students meet both important science curriculum standards and the school's goals of promoting critical
thinking and problem solving. He quickly embraced the students' idea.

One of Roberts's first steps in implementing this project
was to ask his students to help him to devise the various
learning activities for the Recharge the Battery project. So how
did the students and Roberts carry out this inquiry? None of
the students had any real experience with free-range chickens.
So one of these activities was to raise free-range chickens on
the school's grounds and set up a webcam so that they and
anyone else with access to the Web could learn more about
what life was like for these chickens. The students also helped
develop the assessment for the project. They decided to use
the cameras on their cell phones to record their assessments
of their own work and that of other students. Another facet
of their assessment involved their families. The students
shared their conclusions about which form of raising chickens made the most sense with their families and monitored
whether their conclusions changed their families' purchas-
ing habits. Many parents reported that their children's work
convinced them to buy more expensive free-range chicken.
They also began calling the school wondering what was
happening. Their children were actually talking about what
they were learning in school rather than providing single-
syllable answers like "fine," which are common when parents ask about school (D. Roberts, personal communication,
November 2008 and January 2009).

Find your copy of the Learning Activity Checklist, because
this is something you can do at home. Does this project align

with the characteristics of effective learning? Don't read further until you have answered the question. Once you have completed your task, compare your answers with those that follow.

- Is it a standards-based task? The short answer is yes!
- Is it an engaging task? You know the short answer. The somewhat longer answer is that students are actively involved in their learning. They are given choices in what and how they learn. The project clearly has meaning to them and is valued by others in their community outside of school. The students are gathering information, analyzing and synthesizing it, and creating knowledge that they share with others outside the school.
- Is it a problem-based task? Yes. They are solving real problems and trying to convince others to follow their advice.
- Was technology used to enhance student learning? Yes, but it clearly wasn't at the center of this project; 21st-century pedagogy was.

Reviewing this learning activity reveals its goals are dramatically different from those of traditional instruction. Powerful pedagogy makes it effective. Technology is not transforming learning; it is just a tool the students in these activities used to reach the goals of the learning activities.

Pedagogy Needs to Drive Technology Use

Focusing first on pedagogy and learning objectives offers educators an effective strategy to integrate technology into their classrooms. Sylvia Tolisano (2009) frames the rationale for this new approach nicely when she concludes, "It is not (never was) about technology. To make

> It is not (never was) about technology. To make a difference, it has always been about good teaching, reflecting and focusing on (relevant?) student learning. (Sylvia Tolisano, 2009)

a difference, it has always been about good teaching, reflecting and focusing on (relevant?) student learning." Why is this strategy for technology integration more promising? Because it emphasizes teaching and student learning, two issues familiar to educators. We are starting the conversation on the educators' home court, something we could never say when the focus was on technology. This strategy is also consistent with the goal of offering 21st-century learning opportunities to all students.

This approach of using pedagogy to drive the use of ICT is one that is being implemented by some of the world's best school systems. In Finland, for example, "pedagogical models and practices are at the forefront while technological tools are relegated to supporting the educational content." And in Singapore, educators see technology as an aid to "high quality instruction, not in place of it" (Armstrong, 2012b, p. 5).

TECHNOLOGY INTEGRATION REDEFINED

So finally we have a new definition that explains technology integration. **Technology supports and enhances 21st-century pedagogy and content.** What does this definition of technology integration mean for the role of teacher? Several years ago, I worked with a small group of innovative educators Microsoft had gathered from around the world. They concluded that a teacher who was effective at integrating technology focused his or her efforts on creating learning activities that actively engaged students in learning and helped them develop the skills and competencies they needed for future success. The teacher's primary role is to offer learning activities that feature effective content and pedagogy. Notice there is no mention of the word *technology*. These innovative educators insisted that after the teacher created the learning activity, the teacher and his or her students would choose the technology that they felt would be best to accomplish the task outline by the teacher. If there were students in the class who needed help to use this technology, a student who was comfortable with the technology would provide the assistance (L. Foltos, personal notes, June 2009).

Coaching Teachers to Integrate Technology

So how do Peer Coaches fit into this equation? It would be easy to say focus on pedagogy first and technology will enhance instruction. Turning this simple idea into practice requires teachers to have a crystal-clear focus on their instructional goals and the instructional strategies they plan to use to reach these goals. How can Peer Coaches help teachers to develop this focus? Let's explore how one process of emphasizing instructional goals and strategies works to define how technology can be integrated.

So how do Peer Coaches fit into this equation? It would be easy to say focus on pedagogy first and technology will enhance instruction. Turning this simple idea into practice requires teachers to have a crystal-clear focus on their instructional goals and the instructional strategies they plan to use to reach these goals.

Not that long ago, I worked with a group of about 100 leaders from a nearby school district. These were principals, head teachers, and some central district staff. Their goal was to explore effective learning for students and the kind of professional learning that would support it. After the group agreed that the Learning Activity Checklist would serve as a tentative norm for effective instruction, we began to use it by reviewing the project on cleaning up the pollution in the Yamuna River that we reviewed in Chapter 6, so get your notes on this activity out. As the educators suggested ways to make it a more engaging task, some interesting connections among pedagogy, content, and technology began to emerge.

The task for this learning activity asked the students to solve a number of problems. Students needed to learn what was polluting the river and how pollutants affected their health. They were also asked to come up with solutions to mitigate or eliminate the sources of the pollution. Once they had identified what was in the river, eliminating the problem of pollution required the students to find the source. Some of the educators quickly went online and reported that the Yamuna is a long river; it flows through many cities and agricultural areas before it gets to Nitin's hometown. If the students really wanted to solve the problem, these educators recommended the students would have to communicate and collaborate with students in other towns along the river to gather information about the sources of pollution and how to eliminate them. While no one suggested a specific tool that students should use, several educators said students could use email, texts, or social networking software to communicate and collaborate to get the information they needed.

While the educators debated about whether a large collaborative project with schools along the river was realistic, they observed that even if the students in Nitin's school worked with only one additional school, they would need to create some sort of common database for their findings. Once the students had gathered data, the educators observed that the students would need to draw some sort of conclusions from the data about how to deal with the problem. Drawing conclusions, they insisted, meant the students would first have to analyze and synthesize the data they had collected. Again, the educational leaders didn't specify exactly what tool to use, but they did suggest that databases or spreadsheets would make the process much more effective.

These educators also observed that the students had been communicating with doctors and environmental experts to gather information about pollution and its effects. They felt it would be a strong assessment strategy to ask the students to reach out to these experts again to get feedback on the students' tentative conclusions and ask these experts to play some role in assessing the final product of the students' learning. They thought some sort of technology, like email or video conferencing, might be useful in the process of having these real-world experts play a role in both providing feedback and assessing student work.

Finally, the educators who were assessing this environmental project observed that the students were encouraged to print posters to share their findings with their community and encourage their parents, relatives, and others to take action. In addition to these posters, the educators assessing this project suggested the students use websites or videos to reach a broader audience in the community. And they argued that the students could get feedback from the community more effectively if they used some sort of technology like chats, social networking, or text messages to secure that feedback.

By the time I asked them to explore the last quadrant of the Learning Activity Checklist, how could the teacher better use technology to enhance student learning, these educators responded, "We have already done that" (L. Foltos, personal notes, August 2010).

Their discussion focused first and foremost on the kinds of issues that are central to teaching: content and pedagogy. As they looked at ways to make the students' task more engaging, the educators identified the learning objectives. Then they explored ways to help improve the learning activity by rethinking the ways to reach its objectives. As they explored ways to help students more effectively communicate, collaborate, and share the knowledge they had created, these educators were recognizing ways to integrate technology. What is crucial to take away from their experiences is that defining how to integrate technology was a by-product of the discussion of how to achieve the project's learning objectives.

By now, I hope that the tools and processes these educators used feel familiar to you. They should. I didn't reinvent the wheel to facilitate this discussion; I used the same tools and processes that Peer Coaches routinely use as they assist teachers to integrate technology.

PEER COACHING TECHNOLOGY INTEGRATION TOOLKIT

Peer Coaches have a number of potential tools they can use to refocus discussions about technology to emphasize learning goals and instructional strategies the teacher hopes to reach in the learning activity.

Lesson-Improvement Process

If a Peer Coach is coplanning a learning activity with a peer, they follow a process that encourages them to:

- Define a task and standards they want student to achieve
- Outline the process they want students to follow to address the task
- Define an assessment strategy

In short, the Peer Coach and collaborating teacher emphasize powerful pedagogy and effective assessment. Their conversation about integrating technology occurs in the context of achieving specific learning objectives and enhancing teaching strategies the teacher plans to employ. When discussed in this context, technology integration isn't driving instruction; it is an integral part, perhaps a small part, of the overall process of improving a learning activity.

Peeling the Onion

> Getting at the key issues for successful technology integration is like peeling back the layers of an onion one at a time. Peer Coaches peel away the layers of the learning activity until they have exposed what the teacher wants students to know and be able to do.

Mary Lou Ley, who leads Wisconsin's Peer Coaching Collaborative, offers coaches another tool to help teachers integrate technology effectively. Her tool is actually a colorful metaphor. Getting at the key issues for successful technology integration is like peeling back the layers of an onion one at a time. Peer Coaches peel away the layers of the learning activity until they have exposed what the teacher wants students to know and be able to do. If you were looking for an example of how this peeling approach might work, think of the Peer Coaches who looked for tasks like communication, collaboration, gathering or analyzing information, or expression when collaborating with a learning partner. They were peeling back the layers as they looked for these tasks. With this focus on student learning, Peer Coaches have a powerful strategy that they can use to help their colleagues integrate technology effectively (Ley, 2011; M. Ley, personal communication, July 16, 2012). It certainly was a valuable strategy for that group of educators who were discussing the Yamuna River project.

Emphasizing Student Tasks

This idea of peeling away the layers of the onion is totally consistent with the approach we discussed at the start of this chapter. Effective coaches listen and raise questions to determine if their learning partners are asking students to communicate, collaborate, gather and organize information and for how they want students to demonstrate learning. They may, for example, encourage their learning partners to define the purposes of collaboration and who is collaborating and ask them to consider what tools they would suggest to make this collaboration effective. Even when their learning partner meets them in the hallway and asks, "What about using PhotoStory in my biography project?" the coach's job is to bring the conversation back to pedagogy and learning objectives before talking about technology. It is at this point in the process when meaningful conversations about integrating technology occur.

Summary

Coaches must understand that best practices in technology integration are really best practices in 21st-century learning. Technology integration is all about the interrelationship of pedagogy, content, and technology. And technology is the least important of the three elements in this equation. Coaches become effective at helping other teachers integrate technology by:

(Continued)

(Continued)

- Redefining the term *technology integration*
- Collaborating with teachers to help develop relevant techno-fluency
- Using familiar tools and resources to keep technology-integration conversations focused on pedagogy and content. These include:
  - o Giving attention to the lesson-design process
  - o Peeling back the onion to understand the learning goals and instructional strategies the teacher hopes to employ
  - o Emphasizing learning tasks like communication, collaboration, gathering and organizing information, and expression as starting points for discussions about integrating technology

9

Connecting Coaching Skills to Practice

It [my second year coaching] gave me time to really think through a strategy, try some things out and discard what didn't work. It also allowed me time to develop relationships with my fellow peer coaches that will help me.

—Anonymous Peer Coach

As coaches begin to practice their craft, they learn to utilize what they have learned about coaching and come to appreciate what they still need to know to be successful. Nothing increases the demand for more professional learning than a Peer Coach's initial experiences practicing his or her craft. Even limited experience convinces Peer Coaches of the value of conversations with other coaches about what is working, sharing why they are being successful, and discussing coaching challenges and possible solutions. Their initial attempts at observation and reflection lead coaches to want to know more about how to be more effective in this key role. Experienced Peer Coaches understand that a coach's professional learning needs to mirror what we know about effective professional development; it needs to be sustained, intensive, and connected to practice.

LEARNING FROM SUCCESSES AND CHALLENGES

The first cohort of Peer Coaches met after a few months of classroom coaching experience to talk about the successes and challenges they faced. I asked one or two open-ended questions and guided their ensuing discussion. After this conversation, the coaches demanded that these reflections on successes and challenges be more than a seemingly random discussion about issues of immediate interest to the coaches. Instead of free-form reflection, they wanted to structure the discussions, to focus the conversations, to drill deeper into the topics being discussed, and to ensure that coaches had clear ideas they could take away from these activities. To meet these demands, the Peer Coaching curriculum writers created several activities to provide this structure.

> Instead of free-form reflection, they wanted to structure the discussions, to focus the conversations, to drill deeper into the topics being discussed, and to ensure that coaches had clear ideas they could take away from these activities.

The first of these structured activities was constructed around the Atlas Communities' Wows and Wonders protocol, which was designed to discuss both successes and challenges. The protocol was adapted to give speakers the opportunity to outline one aspect of their work in which they had experienced successes and challenges, like sharing their coaching program with educators at their schools or recruiting learning partners (Meyer et al., 2011aa).

Before we explain the activity, let's define the term *protocol*. Dictionary.com tells us a protocol is "the customs and regulations dealing with diplomatic formality, precedence, and etiquette." Or, in medicine, it is a plan for "carrying out a patient's treatment regimen." In either of these cases, a protocol is a carefully prescribed way of doing something. Failure to follow the protocol carefully can have negative consequences. Let me give you a brief, personal, example. I had problem and went to see the doctor. He gave me a prescription to take one pill three times a day for 10 days. This prescription is a protocol. I took the medicine three times a day for 3 days, felt better, and stopped taking the medicine. Two days later I was back in the doctor's office complaining of my original symptoms. The first question out of the doctor's mouth was, "Did you take all of the medicine as directed?" The treatment had failed because I had failed to follow the protocol explicitly. It is just as important for educators to follow protocols closely if they want them to work.

In the Wows and Wonders protocol, speakers present their situations to small groups of coaches. They might, for example share a dilemma like "I am struggling with my desire to work on lesson improvement while my collaborating teachers want help with software." The other coaches listen, ask clarifying questions, and share their *wows*. Wows are what the coaches learned from the presenter and the insights they gained into the issue the presenter is sharing. The listeners also use probing questions to raise *wonders* about what they have heard. Wonders should encourage the presenters to think about their issues from a different perspective. Finally, the presenters reflect on how the wows and the wonders prompted them to think differently about the issues they presented. Their feedback gives the listeners insights into what makes a wow or wonder effective and what they can do to make their coaching more effective (Meyer et al., 2011aa).

Protocols like Wows and Wonders and others created by the National School Reform Faculty are being used in education more and more frequently because protocols give educators a powerful set of tools to guide and shape conversations. They are designed to limit the free flow of ideas that might surface while teachers are using a protocol. They are so prescriptive that many educators feel they impose artificial boundaries on conversations. They do, but there is a valuable trade-off. The Wows and Wonders discussion focused only on what listeners learned from the speakers and their probing questions, which are designed to offer the speakers different perspectives on the issues they chose to share. Peer Coaches at a secondary school outside of Sydney, Australia, feel these limits are the biggest virtue of protocols. These coaches told me they "anchor their conversations in the protocol" because it kept them focused (J. Linklater, P. Hunt, & D. Macleod-Jones, personal communication, June 29, 2012). For protocols to be effective, coaches and other educators need to learn to set aside their initial concerns and use protocols exactly as written.

A second activity for structuring discussions is a tool groups of Peer Coaches use in their efforts to address roadblocks to their success. This tool (see Table 9.1) is designed to provide small groups of coaches a tool for problem solving.

Numerous Peer Coaches have told me that the Wows and Wonders protocol and the Roadblock activity have been important in their success. These tools work because they help Peer Coaches unlock the power of collaboration with a group to get to the roots of what is required for successful coaching. The Roadblock activity, for example, gives groups of Peer Coaches a process for problem solving that they can apply to other vexing issues in the future. Without these tools and shared experiences, coaching can founder.

Collaboration to Improve Learning

Even after several months of experience collaborating with colleagues in their schools, many Peer Coaches may still lack an appreciation of the power collaboration has to improve learning. One strategy to make the relationship between collaboration and improving learning explicit is to ask coaches to discuss an example of a learning activity they have helped another teacher improve and work the students have created while completing this activity. For this activity

Table 9.1   Coaching Roadblocks Template

Define the Problem
■ Gather information; for example, review your collaboration log or talk to your collaborating teacher.
■ Identify relevant facts.
Identify the Causes
■ Discuss possible causes with others.
■ Try putting yourself in the other person's shoes.
■ Think of all the possible causes to the problem.
Generate Possible Solutions
■ Research ideas on the Internet.
■ Ask collaborating teachers and other coaches for ideas.
■ Keep in mind what you can and cannot control.
Decide on a Solution
■ Review the list of suggestions and ideas to identify a solution that will improve the situation.
■ Make sure the solution can be accomplished in the time you can commit to coaching.
■ Make sure the solution is within your control.
Plan
■ Write a goal and a checkpoint to determine if the solution is working.
Identify Action Steps to Solve the Problem

Source: Meyer et al. (2011h).

to work, the participants need to share the work of the best students, average students, and some who clearly didn't do well in this learning activity. If they want a candid discussion of successful collaboration, they have to look beyond success. Coaches form small groups and use the classroom evidence as they participate in a revised version of the Success Analysis Protocol created by the National School Reform Faculty (Meyer et al., 2011y). This focused discussion explores the role collaboration between Peer Coach and learning partner plays in improving student learning. The protocol also encourages coaches to emphasize student work as they reflect on strategies, techniques, and approaches that make collaboration work. Experience with protocols not only offers insights into the value of collaboration and provides a framework to discuss coaching but also is critical for success in another facet of coaching: observing a peer and reflecting afterward.

OBSERVATION

The first step toward any successful observation is for the coach and his or her learning partner to agree to the overarching goal for any observation. Long before they set a date for an observation, the collaborating teacher and coach need to agree that their goal in this activity is to explore what the learning activity intends and what the students are saying, doing, and learning. In other words, they will be focusing on how the learners respond to the learning activity, not to the teacher. The reason that this is a critical first step is rooted in the culture of schools.

Focus on the Learners

Linda Darling-Hammond and colleagues (2009) have observed that the simplest way to break down the isolation that separates teachers is to observe colleagues and to provide constructive feedback, but it is rare to see American teachers use this simple approach. When teachers do observe each other, researchers have concluded that the conversations based on these observations often come straight from the "culture of nice." "Nice" discussions feature vague compliments about what a good job the presenting teacher did and avoid anything that might be seen as a criticism (City et al., 2009; MacDonald, 2011). These nice conversations have stultifying effects on meaningful exploration of teaching practice. Since they steer clear of challenging beliefs or practices, there is little or no chance they will encourage innovation. On the surface, they seem to be a step toward collaboration, but City and colleagues (2009) insist that these conversations reflect a culture in which "one's practice is one's private property and not a collective good" (p. 164). The culture of "nice" isn't limited to the United States. Based on my international experiences, I think it is fairly pervasive in schools around the world.

Nice conversations also pose another problem. When a reflective conversation talks about teachers who did a good job, that discussion is off to a really bad start. In fact, the only way it could be worse is if the educators started by saying something like, "Joan did a really good job in that lesson today." Now the conversation is about Joan and is focused on Joan's personal strengths and weaknesses. Teachers who are nice want to be polite and to stay away from controversy. But if the conversation veers toward a real, meaningful reflection of whether Joan's lesson really helped students reach its goals, any critical comments are focused on Joan and are by definition personal. Remember, effective coaches discuss ideas, not people. By focusing on the individual, educators are robbing themselves of one strategy that might produce improvements in teaching and learning.

> When a reflective conversation talks about teachers who did a good job, that discussion is off to a really bad start.

There are strategies coaches can use to shape meaningful reflection on teaching and learning and maintain their personal and professional relationships with their peers. One observation strategy is for the coach to focus on what the students are doing, saying, and learning. This approach recognizes the fact that student learning offers the easiest avenue to assess the successes of a learning activity. Mary Lou

> Any reflective conversation between a Peer Coach and collaborating teacher needs to be focused on evidence about teaching and learning. Ley (2011) asserts that evidence is found by exploring student work because it "provides concrete evidence of what the teacher intended and what the student learned."

Ley, who leads Wisconsin's Peer Coaching Collaborative, insists that any reflective conversation between a Peer Coach and collaborating teacher needs to be focused on evidence about teaching and learning. Ley (2011) asserts that evidence is found by exploring student work because it "provides concrete evidence of what the teacher intended and what the student learned." The authors of *Instructional Rounds* (City et al., 2009) are strong advocates for placing the emphasis in any observation on the students. City and her coauthors (2009) note that they often hear educators talk about how the lesson went without discussing what students were actually doing and the evidence of what students actually knew as a result of the teaching. To make observations effective, City's team encourages those observing during instructional rounds to look at what students are saying and doing rather than at the teacher.

What do Ley's ideas and this research tell coaches? If Peer Coaches want the observation to produce meaningful reflective discussion, coaches should focus on what students are doing, saying, and learning during the observation, and that emphasis on student learning should shape the reflection that follows. These ideas should also produce a broader insight that is critical for successful coaching. Peer Coaches need to act on the understanding that meaningful professional learning comes from discussing student learning, not what the teacher did right or wrong.

Preobservation Meetings

The coach and collaborating teacher typically meet prior to the observation to establish the goals for the observation. Even if the coach coplanned the activity, it is still important for the coach and teacher to decide on the goals of the observation. Classroom observations need not last for hours. Many effective observations are completed in less than 30 minutes, some far less. Shorter may be good in many respects, but shorter also makes it more critical to define the purpose of the observation. Will the coach be looking for evidence of student creativity, effective collaboration, or the use of formative assessment strategies? In a presentation on Peer Coaching at the ISTE conference in 2012, Mary Lou Ley shared one tool (see Table 9.2) that Peer Coaches and collaborating teachers could use to define the purpose of the observation. It focuses on how revisions to a learning activity, made by the teacher and coach, affect student learning.

Another goal of these preobservation meetings is to be clear about what tool or rubric the coach and teacher will use to discuss the observation. Since Peer Coaches and their colleagues typically use their norm for effective learning, the Learning Activity Checklist, as they improve the activity, some portion of the Checklist is commonly used as a rubric to guide the conversation after the observation.

EFFECTIVE REFLECTION

Collaborative Norms

I encourage the coach and collaborating teacher to review their norms for collaboration before any reflective discussion to ensure their norms guide the conversation. Norms like discussing issues, not people, showing respect for the views of others, and presuming positive intentions are critical for a productive discussion of what occurred during the

Table 9.2   Reflection Tool

	Elements of original activity	What changed? What was revised?	Impact on student learning?
Before observation			
During observation			

Source: M. L. Ley, personal communication, June 26, 2012.

observation. As Garmston and Wellman (1999) note, a norm like presuming positive intentions reinforces the idea that all the participants in the discussion have the same goals and reduces the possibility that the listener will see probing questions as a threat. This brief review of the norms of collaboration serves as a reminder for both the coach and the collaborating teacher that they will use their norms to shape an honest conversation by focusing on the learning activity and what the students were doing and learning, not on the teacher.

Video and Observation

The authors of "Record, Replay, Reflect" (Knight et al., 2012) suggest that video can be a particularly powerful tool when used as part of the process of reflection. "Cameras can help educators...obtain an objective, accurate view of themselves at work" (p. 19). Those Peer Coaches who use video tell me that this resource eliminates confusion and disagreements about what the teacher or the students really said. Reviewing the video wipes out all doubts about what was said and done. And, as Knight's group (2012) concluded, observing video recordings helps coaches and the teachers they work with measure progress toward their goals and identify the activities and strategies that are most effective at increasing student engagement.

The Power of Protocols

Earlier we talked about one use for the Wows and Wonders and Success Analysis protocols, but Peer Coaches quickly recognize another powerful use. After their preliminary experience using each of these protocols, Peer Coaches discuss how they might use the protocol in other ways. Invariably they conclude that both of the protocols would provide structure for the reflective conversation that follows a classroom observation of a peer. Using protocols, they insist, keeps the reflection between teacher and coach safe because protocols focus the discussion on learning activities and student learning, not on the teacher. Researchers agree that protocols that limit discussions to the learning activity provide safety because they separate teaching practice from the person who created or taught the activity (City et al., 2009; Garmston, 2005). Protocols have proven so effective that they should be the primary tools coaches use in reflective discussions following a classroom observation.

Feedback

Effective coaches draw on a variety of skills they have learned to provide feedback. Earlier we noted that coaches use their norm for effective learning to shape the feedback they offer. Many protocols like Wows and Wonders and the Success Analysis Protocol are also shaped in ways that require the coach to use communication skills, like paraphrasing and probing questions. The authors of these protocols understand that paraphrasing and probing questions are particularly useful tools for providing effective feedback. These skills are designed to encourage reflection and prompt innovation. In their book *Coaching Conversations*, Gross Cheliotes and Reilly (2010) encourage coaches to use reflective questions, which are similar to probing questions, because they provide feedback that "engages the other person in deep reflection and possibility thinking" (p. 69).

I do everything I can to encourage inquiry over advocacy, but once the coaching relationship is well established, the coach is likely to offer advice or make suggestions. This form of feedback needs to be shaped by the same philosophy that guides probing questions. Suggestions and advice should be strategies coaches use occasionally. When they do provide advice, it should be limited to a few ideas that the learning partner can act on. This approach to feedback maintains the relationship between peers as equals and continues to encourage the learning partner to take responsibility for applying what he or she learns in collaboration with the coach.

ONGOING PROFESSIONAL LEARNING

After reviewing evaluations of the Peer Coaching program in Washington State, it is clear that these coaches understand that much of their success as coaches comes from what they learn on the job. Many Peer Coaches report they feel somewhat overwhelmed as they start coaching peers, but they feel much more effective after a year or more of classroom coaching experience. As one coach observed,

> In year one you are still trying to figure it all out, putting things into action... but year two allows you to step back and reflect on the growth of year one, breathe and then move forward. Student learning in year two was definitely impacted more because I knew what worked from year one. (Liston & Ragan, 2010, p. 60)

Other coaches reported that after a year of coaching, they were setting more achievable goals, feeling more at home as coaches, and felt more effective at using communications skills, using collaborative tools like protocols, and building trusting relationships (Liston & Ragan, 2010). Clearly, on-the-job experience helps. The experiences of these Peer Coaches from Washington are consistent with what I hear from Peer Coaches around the country and around the world. They routinely tell me that after the formal Peer Coach training and at least a year of experience coaching, they are beginning to feel like they are mastering the art of coaching.

Conversations with these coaches make it clear that they also understand that the development of their coaching skills is an ongoing process. After coaches complete formal training, much of their professional learning is defined by their coaching experiences. These experiences lead coaches to look for ways to sharpen their craft and meet their needs. Some of the kinds of professional learning they pursue include:

- Facilitators in Washington State offer coaches a second year of formal training that emphasizes technology integration, developing more collaboration skills, or rethinking and revising their coaching plans as they gain experience.

Forrest Fischer, from Yakima, goes a step further and asks experienced coaches to join the relative newcomers to the coaching ranks in these sessions. This collaboration among coaches with differing levels of experience draws heavily on the experiences of seasoned coaching veterans, and it strengthens the skills of all of the coaches.

- Some Peer Coaches choose to enroll in training for *Understanding by Design* so that they can improve their lesson-design skills. Others may enroll in programs like Cognitive Coaching to enhance their communication and collaboration skills.

- Mary Lou Ley, a facilitator in Wisconsin, offers coaches the opportunity to enroll in a second year of training. Some of this training emphasizes the further development of communication skills so that the coaches are more effective at driving innovation and encouraging peers to take more risks to improve learning.

While many coaches around the world rely on formal professional-learning experiences aimed at developing and refining their coaching skills, they also draw on the power of collaboration to reach those goals. *Collaboration* isn't simply more educational jargon or empty rhetoric for these coaches. They have learned that collaboration was the key to their initial successes and to their further development as coaches. The ways they collaborate to continue to foster their learning take on wildly different forms.

> *Collaboration* isn't simply more educational jargon or empty rhetoric for these coaches. They have learned that collaboration was the key to their initial successes and to their further development as coaches. The ways they collaborate to continue to foster their learning take on wildly different forms.

- Tracy Watanabe in Apache Junction, Arizona, uses blog posts to record and share coaching success in schools across her school district. These efforts build community and facilitate sharing among Peer Coaches in schools across the district (T. Watanabe, personal communication, May 22, 2012).

- Jenny Linklater has formed the six Peer Coaches at her school into a professional learning community that meets often to discuss coaching, share successes, and address the challenges each coach faces (J. Linklater, personal communication, June 14, 2012).
- Coaches from across Lithuania met in a nationwide Peer Coaching conference to learn from one another and to get insights into coaching from Peer Coaches from the Ukraine and Sweden who join the meeting using Skype.
- Educators from Sweden, the United States, and Australia have joined scheduled "Tweetfests" to discuss ways to improve their coaching skills.
- The Northern Arizona branch of AzTEA, the Arizona Technology in Education Association, has held two statewide coaching conferences to encourage discussions about communication, lesson design, and supporting and sustaining coaching. Participants had the choice of joining these discussions face to face or online using AzTEA's Web conferencing software.
- Coaches also come together in birds-of-a-feather meetings at regional and international conferences, like the ISTE (International Society for Technology in Education) conferences.
- Coaches in Washington State and Victoria, Australia, have collaborated using a variety of online tools and in at least one face-to-face meeting since 2005.
- Coaches in the UK, Australia, and the United States share their learning with peers on YouTube.
- In 2012, the PLANE program in New South Wales began to offer Peer Coaches from across the state the opportunity to meet and learn in a virtual coaching world. PLANE is a valuable resource for each of these coaches, but it is particularly important to the growing number of Peer Coaches who work at remote schools and have few chances for collaboration. This virtual coaching world provides them with opportunities to collaborate and learn with and from Peer Coaches from across the state (PLANE, n.d.).

Whether Peer Coaches connect face to face or via Web conferencing software, email, or Twitter, what is critical to note is that they aren't participating because they have to. They volunteer because they understand they need to continue to expand their coaching skills to meet the needs of both their learning partners and their students. And they understand the power of collaboration for professional learning. They volunteer, and in some cases pay, for these learning opportunities because they insist that collaboration with other coaches is the most effective way to further their education and improve their practice as coaches.

Summary

Training for coaches needs to follow what we know about effective professional learning. It must be intensive, sustained, and connected to practice.

- Coaches want and need structured conversations to learn from one another about successes and challenges. The structure focuses the conversation, making it more effective at providing ideas the coaches can bring back to their schools and use.
- Coaches cannot fall into the culture of "nice" and expect meaningful results. They need to use strategies to separate discussion of the learning activity and student learning from the person who created and taught it.
- Prior to any classroom observation, coaches should meet with their learning partners to set goals, review their norms for collaboration, and discuss strategies to defuse potential conflicts in their discussion of the observation.
- Coaches need to learn to use protocols to shape reflective discussions after classroom observation. Protocols keep reflective discussions focused and safe.
- In reflective conversations following observations, the Peer Coach's job is to peel away topics or issues that get in the way of discussing student work.
- No matter how much formal training they experience, coaches around the world report that ongoing, on-the-job professional learning is critical to their success.

10

Sustaining Coaching and Building Capacity

Above all use collective capacity as the foundation of innovative teaching and learning work.

—Michael Fullan (2011b)

One critical element of implementing educational innovation is sustaining that innovation by providing long-term support. In an age when school principals and particularly school district leaders seem to come and go with the season, long-term support seems like a rare commodity. Those of us in education know why ongoing support for reform programs is essential. Every leader seems to have an agenda. No one seems to want to continue a predecessor's programs. We have all seen many educational initiatives start, burn brightly, and then burn out completely because they lack long-term support. After experiencing this cycle a few times, the effect is similar to the death of a star. The educational equivalent of a black hole forms, and you can almost feel the failure of yet another reform movement suck the willingness to adopt any new reforms out of teachers. So what does it take to implement and sustain an effective coaching program?

IMPLEMENTING PEER COACHING: THE BASICS

In Chapter 4, we explored a few of the essentials needed to launch a coaching program successfully. They included:

- Choose schools that believe that improving student learning depends on shared leadership and on ongoing, highly collaborative professional learning.
- Choose the right teacher leaders to be coaches.
- Start with the teachers who are willing to collaborate to improve their teaching and student learning.
- Create a Coaching Plan to align coaching with school goals and programs, provide resources critical to the success of coaching, and assess the success of coaching.
- Share the results of coaching activities early and often.
- Integrate the Coaching Plan into the school's educational plan and routinely review and revise it to ensure it meets school needs.

With these essentials in place, most schools are ready to launch a coaching program. But is this enough to sustain coaching over time? Maybe. Most of this book has emphasized the collaborative relationship between a Peer Coach and a teacher. This has allowed us to explore a series of attributes, skills, strategies, and resources that make a coach successful. Ultimately, the success of one coach and one teacher provides the paramount reason to sustain coaching. As important as individual successes are, we need to broaden our perspective to understand the other factors required to sustain coaching.

Peer Coaching: Expense vs. Investment

Ultimately, the decision to continue to support coaching may rest on whether the school's educators perceive coaching as an expense or as an investment in building the school's capacity to improve teaching and learning. School and school district leaders from around the world

> Ultimately, the decision to continue to support coaching may rest on whether the school's educators perceive coaching as an expense or as an investment in building the school's capacity to improve teaching and learning.

have told me that coaching is cost effective. But it isn't free. In addition to ongoing staffing costs, schools provide coaches with time to model, team-teach, observe a peer teach, and then reflect afterward. Typically, this means the schools needs to fund a substitute teacher to provide this time. In an age when school budgets are shrinking so dramatically that principals start the back-to-school meeting by asking parents to supply paper for the school's copy machines, why would a school want to continue to fund coaching?

I have often heard Vincent Quah, an educational leader in Singapore, urge educators from around the world to invest in their schools' human infrastructure, its educators. Peer Coaching is the kind of investment he talks about, because Peer Coaches help build their school's capacity to improve teaching and learning. What does capacity building look like? It includes:

- Coaches who help teachers use a lesson-improvement process to work toward implementing a norm for effective learning
- Coaches who assist teachers to use a variety of communication and collaboration skills and tools to make collaboration more effective
- Collaborating teachers who continue to create learning activities based on the ideas, insights, and strategies they developed while working with their coach
- The ripple effect that occurs when a collaborating teacher works with a coach one day and the next day

turns to other peers and models collaboration skills as he or she shares lessons learned with and from the coach

BUILDING SUPPORT TO BUILD CAPACITY

How can coaching avoid becoming another small-scale, short-lived educational experiment? How does it become central to other school plans for success and part of the school's plan to build capacity to improve teaching and learning? And what roles do the coach and the principal play in this process of creating support for coaching?

School Leadership

The improvements in teaching and learning I have seen in the classrooms of teachers who collaborate with Peer Coaches are incredible. But there are clear limits to a coach's powers. Coaches working with one or two colleagues may create a small-scale success working in the margins in their schools. Building schoolwide coaching programs is something they can't do alone. They need the support of their schools' principals and their colleagues. I have already talked a bit about the successes of Peer Coaching at Dallas Primary School near Melbourne, Australia; telling a bit more of the school's story should define the role of the principal to the success of coaching.

When Valerie Karaitiana became the principal at Dallas several years ago, the school had some of the worst test scores in the state. Its students overwhelmingly came from dire economic circumstances, and few spoke English at home. She and her leadership team decided that one solution to improve learning was to emphasize collaboration. Today, when you walk into any classroom in Dallas, it is clear that collaboration is part of daily life for students and teachers. There are constant collaborative conversations going on between students, between students and educators, and between educators.

You can almost feel the learning happening around you. When you talk to the school's leaders, they will tell you that the school's six Peer Coaches played a key role in helping educators learn to collaborate and improve their practice. In fact, they insist that Peer Coaches have played a central role in building the school's capacity to improve teaching and learning and the school's test scores, which are now near the midpoint for schools across the state. Let's take a closer look at responsibility (V. Karaitiana & L. Gunning, personal communication, April 5, 2010, June 18, 2010, August 5, 2011).

Karaitiana and her assistant principals, Lynne Gunning and Amanda Henning, set the expectation that all teachers would collaborate with coaches to improve teaching and learning. The principal allocated money in the budget for coach training and the time for teachers to collaborate regularly with one of the school's coaches. In addition, the principal assigned Peer Coaches an active role in each of the school's professional learning communities, and they are an integral part of the school's Instructional Rounds program. Collaboration with a Peer Coach is still expected, but today teachers seek out coaches and ask to collaborate. Teachers tell visitors that coaching has helped them improve their practice and student learning. But the coaches all quickly point out that their success rested on the vision, guidance, and support of the principal and assistant principals. This interdependent relationship between the school's formal leaders and its coaches is one of the keys to a school's efforts to build capacity for innovation (V. Karaitiana & L. Gunning, personal communication, April 5, 2010, June 18, 2010, August 5, 2011).

> This interdependent relationship between the school's formal leaders and its coaches is one of the keys to a school's efforts to build capacity for innovation (V. Karaitiana & L. Gunning, personal communication, April 5, 2010, June 18, 2010, August 5, 2011).

Dallas's story is unique in many respects, but in other ways it is similar to those of other schools with successful coaching programs. Coaches who have been successful at building and sustaining support for Peer Coaching clearly understand the link between their success and active leadership and support from their schools' leadership.

Communicating About Coaching

As I visit schools and talk to school leaders, it is clear that many of them understand that collaboration among teachers is a key to improving learning. But most of these leaders are fairly vague about how to turn that understanding into meaningful practice in their schools. Effective coaches can bridge this gap and may need to take the lead to do so. Their successes may wither on the vine, and coaching may never become more than some small educational experiment if coaches fail to communicate about their coaching work with the school's leaders and staff. In an earlier chapter, we noted that regular communications are the key to creating support and sustaining coaching. Communication is particularly powerful if the coach and his or her learning partner make the link between their work and school goals explicit for school leaders and reach out to share this information with other educators in the school. More and more, I am seeing coaches and collaborating teachers blog or use other online tools to share specific aspects of their collaborative activities, and they encourage other educators at their schools to go online to join the discussion about improving teaching and learning.

Vision Building

One of the goals for Peer Coaching is to help schools develop the capacity to meet their professional-development needs. As we created Peer Coaching, we wanted to see coaching grow to be more than a series of isolated one-on-one relationships in schools, and we believed that Peer Coaching could be part of a broader schoolwide effort to improve teaching and learning. Making coaching part of a broader effort often requires helping educators develop a vision of what effective professional learning means for a school.

Kruse, Louis, and Bryk's (1994) seminal article "Building Professional Community in Schools" was a powerful tool to shape that vision and make a connection between coaching and broader schoolwide professional learning. Kruse and colleagues insisted that effective professional communities demonstrated five critical traits:

1. Reflective dialogue

2. Deprivatization of practice

3. Collective focus on student learning

4. Collaboration

5. Shared norms and values (p. 3)

By this point, the link between coaching and these traits should be clear, but you have read this book. Mike McMann, who was the curriculum director for Seattle Schools, used these five traits to create Standards for Effective School-Based Professional Development. Peer Coach training uses these standards to help principals and coaches gain insights into effective school-based professional learning and to see the link between Peer Coaching and schoolwide efforts to build capacity to improve teaching and learning. Together, principals and coaches review the standards and view a video of a school that is putting these standards into practice to gain insight into what effective professional development might look like in their school. They also discuss how Peer Coaching is aligned with this model for professional development. Other training activities help principals and Peer Coaches assess how their school compares to these standards of effective professional development and begin to build an action plan to move closer to this model of effective professional learning (Meyer et al., 2011l).

School leaders act on their understanding of how coaching could help their school build capacity in a number of different ways. Let's explore three avenues that Peer Coaches and their school leaders have followed to link coaching to broader schoolwide efforts to improve teaching and learning.

BUILDING CAPACITY TO IMPROVE TEACHING AND LEARNING AND BUILD SUPPORT

More Peer Coaches

One of the most frequently implemented strategies to build capacity for improving teaching and learning is to increase the number of coaches at the school. At a secondary school in Western Sydney, the 2012 school year began with six Peer Coaches, three of whom were in formal leadership positions at the school. With the support of the principal, the Peer Coaches introduced coaching to the entire school staff in a day-long workshop that used some of the Peer Coach training activities. As a result of this meeting, the six Peer Coaches collaborated with approximately one-third of the staff at the school. It didn't take long before success stories began "rippling out" from the initial group of Peer Coaches and their learning partners (J. Linklater, P. Hunt, & D. Macleod-Jones, personal communication, June 29, 2012). Buy-in for Peer Coaching expanded like the ripples.

> One of the most frequently implemented strategies to build capacity for improving teaching and learning is to increase the number of coaches at the school.

As the year progressed and coaches and teachers began reporting on their progress, the principal recognized the work of coaches and their learning partners at staff meetings. Jenny Linklater, a Peer Coach and executive teacher responsible for teaching and learning, led a discussion at one of these staff meetings about the importance of collegial dialogue to initiate and sustain improvement in teaching and learning. At another staff meeting, Linklater asked each Peer Coach to lead a small group of teachers in activities designed to help teachers work collaboratively to improve learning activities. Each of the Peer Coaches used the Learning Activity Checklist to build a common set of expectations for effective teaching and learning and guided the teachers' efforts to improve learning activities (J. Linklater, personal communication,

June 14, 2012). Less than a year after the first coaches began collaborating with peers, leadership and staff buy-in to Peer Coaching was broad enough that the school made the decision to invest in Peer Coach training for another cohort of seven teachers. This supportive network of 13 Peer Coaches will help to ensure the school will continue to build the capacity to improve teaching and learning. It isn't hard to imagine the time when every teacher in the school will be able to collaborate with a Peer Coach routinely. This model of building support by building capacity is one I often hear Peer Coaches describe.

Creating a Norm for Effective Learning

Michael Fullan (2011b) insists that one of the main elements in systemic educational reform is "a declared focus on concrete . . . describable innovative teaching practices" (p. 38). In the terms we have been using, that would mean the school's educators explicitly agree to use a norm, like the Learning Activity Checklist, as their goal for improving teaching and learning. We have described how Peer Coaches use the Learning Activity Checklist to guide their work with individual teachers, but this resource may also become a norm to drive improvement for the school's entire staff.

> We have described how Peer Coaches use the Learning Activity Checklist to guide their work with individual teachers, but this resource may also become a norm to drive improvement for the school's entire staff.

Tracy Watanabe was working with a school that was adopting a 1:1 computing program, and she and the school's principal wanted to make sure the staff understood how to use active, engaging learning to make these new tools for learning effective. To help shape this understanding, Watanabe had educators develop a norm for effective instruction. The teachers in this school all had some experience with project-based learning, so Watanabe asked each of them to think about the most successful learning activity they had offered students and, more specifically, what made it successful. Then she asked these educators to get into small groups, share their ideas, and record each of the unique traits on sticky notes. Finally, she gave the whole group a blank version of the Learning Activity Checklist, like Table 10.1 but with a lot more white space, and she asked the groups to put their sticky notes in the quadrant that was most relevant. By the end of the activity, the teachers had created their own Learning Activity Checklist, and as Watanabe said, they "end up owning that activity checklist, because they have essentially created it collectively" (T. Watanabe, personal communication, August 22, 2012).

After they created this checklist, the school's staff then practiced using their norm to assess the strength of a learning activity and make suggestions for improving it. Watanabe also introduced teachers to the Peer Coaching lesson-improvement process to guide their work as they improved lessons. Since the school's Peer Coaches worked with the small groups throughout these activities, it was easy for Watanabe to encourage teachers to continue to collaborate with the coaches to improve learning activities throughout the school year.

Kelli Etheredge, who is a facilitator, Peer Coach, and teacher in Mobile, Alabama, won the support of her school's leadership to help educators create and use a norm for effective learning. She too used training activities from the Peer Coaching curriculum and worked with the majority of the school's teachers to create the school's norm for effective learning. This was just the first step in the process of building capacity to improve teaching and learning. After this activity, she worked with these educators for 2 more full days using this norm and the lesson-improvement process discussed in

Table 10.1   Learning Activity Checklist

Standards-Based Task	Engaging Task
Problem-Based Task	Technology Enhances Learning

Source: Reeder, 2002, in Meyer et al. (2011n).

Chapter 7 to improve a learning activity they would use with students. Her school has 12 Peer Coaches, so teachers have someone that can assist them to adapt and adopt other learning activities that can be shared among teachers working at the same grade level or subject area (K. Etheredge, personal communication, September 17, 2012).

Once a school has a norm for effective learning in place, the school can use the norm to build its collective capacity to improve teaching and learning. The norm facilitates collaboration among the school's teachers by setting an expectation for what learning should look like and helping educators to develop a common language. Educators can use this common language as they discuss how to improve learning activities or as they reflect after they observe each other teach. The norm creates conditions that make it more practical for a coach to work with grade-level or subject-matter teams. If coaches are looking for ways to support and sustain their coaching efforts by building capacity, helping the school to create and use a norm for effective learning is an incredibly powerful tool to secure schoolwide buy-in for coaching.

Peer Coaches and Professional Learning Communities

Linking coaching to a school's professional learning communities (PLCs) can also be incredibly powerful for both coaches and their schools. Principals in many schools act on this understanding by asking coaches to participate in professional learning communities. Peer Coaches can help a learning community adopt and use a norm for effective learning. In many schools, Peer Coaches also help peers in the PLC learn to use communications and collaboration tools to plan and discuss learning activities. At schools like Dallas Primary, Peer

Coaches turn the ideas being discussed in the PLCs into practice by stepping into the classroom to help peers adopt these ideas (V. Karaitiana & L. Gunning, personal communication, August 5, 2011).

If you explore schools that have followed any one of the three avenues for building schoolwide capacity that I just described, you will see that capacity building and support for coaching feed off of one another and fuel an upward spiral of continuous improvement in teaching and learning.

PEER COACHING AND CULTURE

What we have just been describing are some of the ways a Peer Coach can help to create an ecosystem that helps teachers throughout the school to improve teaching and learning. You might call this ecosystem a culture of collaboration. Throughout the book, I have suggested coaches can shape a school's culture by fostering collaboration, modeling the idea of leadership coming from many levels in the school, and playing the role of catalyst in professional learning communities. Since a culture of collaboration is essential to successful schoolwide coaching programs and coaches have often played prominent roles in collaboration, many educators ask if Peer Coaches can create a culture of collaboration in their schools. If you think back to our discussion of the role of the school leadership in supporting and sustaining coaching, it should be clear that changing a school's culture is something that coaches cannot do on their own. Given all of these requirements for transforming school culture, it should be clear that while coaches can provide important leadership for the school, at best they are key players in a school's cultural transformation. The school needs formal leaders that are committed to defining and implementing a culture of collaboration focused on continuous improvement of teaching and learning.

"It's a System Thing, Not a Single Thing"

Throughout this book, I have chosen to focus on individual coaches working with individual teachers and, to a lesser extent, on strategies to expand coaching schoolwide. In essence, I have described elements of bottom-up educational reform. Researchers like Mourshed, Barber, Elmore, and Fullan, who focus on systemic educational reform, make it clear that if schools really want to support, sustain, and maximize the impact of coaching, the focus can't only be on individuals or even on individual schools but must be aimed at school systems. Bottom-up reform must be accompanied by top-down reform, and both must be focused on the same vision (Barber & Mourshed, 2007; Elmore, 2004; Fullan, 2011a, 2011b; Mourshed et al., 2010). In other words, if we are serious about improving schools, we should also be emphasizing the role that the school district plays in driving reform efforts like Peer Coaching.

> Bottom-up reform must be accompanied by top-down reform, and both must be focused on the same vision.

Many school districts are implementing Peer Coaching throughout every school in the district. There are several traits that all of these districts have in common. They have buy-in and support from the district's senior leadership. Each of these districts first aligned Peer Coaching with district goals. All of these districts have at least one facilitator, so they can train coaches to meet district coaching needs, and these facilitators also play key roles in supporting the work of the coaches. They have all built communities of coaches from across their network of schools to utilize the power of collaboration among the coaches. Finally, each of these districts has provided ongoing training, support, and some resources to support and sustain school-based coaches. Let's look at three districts a little more closely to get some insights into how they use Peer Coaching for systemic improvement.

Edmonds School District's Peer Coaching Experience

When she initially adopted Peer Coaching in 2002, Kim Mathey, the instructional technology manager in the Edmonds School District, began to plan to implement Peer Coaching in every school across the district. She worked with the district's leaders to arrange presentations on Peer Coaching for all district principals and other administrators so they had clear insights into coaching and how it could help them reach their goals. Mathey also provided resources like technology and funding for up to 10 days of release time for coaches and teachers to collaborate. Mathey soon recruited an experienced Peer Coach, Lori Soderberg, to become a facilitator who could train coaches in every school and provide ongoing support for these coaches. Mathey and Soderberg also began to share coaching successes at administrators' meetings by asking coaches and their collaborating teachers to present about their experiences at the district's school board meetings.

They gathered coaches from across the district four times a year to provide Peer Coaches opportunities to share and learn from one another and to build the district's collective capacity to use coaching to reach district goals. In addition, these sessions provided coaches with ongoing professional learning. For example, Mathey and Soderberg asked a district literacy specialist to join one of these districtwide coach meetings and share ways that teachers could use mind-mapping software to reach district literacy goals. Prepared with this training, coaches could support teachers' efforts to include this software in classroom activities.

Budget cuts in recent years have limited the district's ability to support coaching activities. The district now provides 3 release days for in-school coaching collaboration each year, and Mathey can bring all the district's coaches together just three times per year. To provide this level of support, she had to reduce the number of coaches. It wasn't something she was comfortable with, but Mathey insisted she did so because she felt it was a "must" to provide successful coaches with ongoing support. Her team continues to provide coaches with ongoing support and to align coaching with district goals. Recently, for example, the district revised the roles of teacher librarians, and Mathey's team is working to train every teacher librarian to step into the role of Peer Coach (K. Mathey, personal communication, August 23, 2012).

Peer Coaching in Flagstaff

After piloting coaching in a couple of schools, Mary Knight, the technology director for Flagstaff Unified School District, wanted to bring Peer Coaching to each school across her district. Starting with a state grant that funded the training of facilitators, she launched training for Peer Coaches in her district and five smaller rural districts in the area in 2007. Her goal was to have coaches in every school across her district, and over time she hopes to have a coach working with the collaborative teams at each grade level and department. Knight also works to ensure coaching is aligned with other district priorities. Flagstaff's coaches are assisting in the implementation of Common Core State Standards and support their colleagues in the effective use of technology for instruction. And Knight and her team worked with the district's curriculum specialists to create iREAD, a program that weaves together pedagogy, content, and iPads to help elementary students reach state literacy goals by the time they complete third grade. Coaching and collaboration are an integral part of iREAD, and Knight's team trained a group of about 15 Peer Coaches to support iREAD.

Knight has used this alignment between Peer Coaching and the district's curricular goals to reach beyond traditional sources of technology funding. She secured Title II funds and some state professional-development resources to fund coach training and provide Peer Coaches with a small stipend. In addition, the district uses its community-supported capital funding to provide coaches with hardware like iPads, Apple TVs, interactive whiteboards, and document cameras as incentives to participate in coaching. The district also funds two facilitators on Knight's team to provide ongoing support and training for coaches. Knight has worked to support Flagstaff's Peer Coaches by providing them with opportunities to attend conferences and workshops, like the Shift-up Conference sponsored by AzTEA, to bring Flagstaff's coaches into the broader national and international coaching community and help Flagstaff's coaches sharpen their skills.

Knight knows that the support she receives from the district is critical to the success of coaching. Her ongoing communications about what's happening with coaches are designed to make sure district-level conversations include Peer Coaching. She and her team work to ensure that principals are in this communication loop and work one on one with principals to define the principals' professional goals for their staffs and look for ways that coaching can support these efforts. The goal of this communication effort is to ensure principals don't see coaching as something extra but as a "foundational piece in accomplishing the school's goals" (M. Knight, personal communication, August 23 and 27, 2012). Knight took several other steps to build the support of principals. She enrolled several principals in Peer Coach training, and they have supported other principals to be more effective instructional leaders in the use of technology. Some of these principals have used coaching skills as they work to improve instruction in their schools. The principals who were trained as coaches also developed a much deeper understanding of the power of coaching and provide strong support for coaching in their schools.

> The goal of this communication effort is to ensure principals don't see coaching as something extra but as a "foundational piece in accomplishing the school's goals" (M. Knight, personal communication, August 23 and 27, 2012).

Apache Junction and Peer Coaching

Tracy Watanabe, a technology integration specialist with the Apache Junction School District, encouraged her district leaders to adopt Peer Coaching because she felt it aligned perfectly with her district's focus on creating 21st-century classrooms that emphasized rigor, relevance, and relationships. Peer Coaches, she thought, could also support the district's efforts to expand its 1:1 laptop program by assisting teachers' use of technology in project-based learning activities. About the time Watanabe and the district's technology director launched a districtwide Peer Coaching program, a new superintendent, who believes in shared leadership and encourages collaboration, joined the district. Watanabe recognized that coaches could play a key role in helping the superintendent reach his goal of creating a culture of collaboration. To align coaching with this goal, Peer Coaches became "Collaboration Coaches" (T. Watanabe, personal communication, July 8, 2011).

From the start, the district played a leading role in the coaching program. Watanabe launched the program by sharing a brochure that outlined a districtwide implementation plan with principals and key district staff. The implementation plan had the district pay coaches to participate in summertime training, and Watanabe has trained 54 coaches who work in all seven of the district's schools. District funds also provide some substitutes so that coaches and teachers can be freed to collaborate (T. Watanabe, personal communication, August 14, 2012). Watanabe spends half of her time in schools supporting coaches and principals and the remainder of her time supporting the Collaboration Coaches in other ways. While she is in schools, Watanabe may be observing teachers and coaches working, and she always leaves a wow and a wonder for those she observes. And she is always looking for examples of effective coaching, teaching, and learning that support the district goals so she can share them with educators across the district (T. Watanabe, personal communication, August 13, 2012).

When she is not in the schools supporting coaches, Watanabe routinely communicates about coaching with the superintendent, principals, the technology director, and others in the district's educational services groups. In one of her conversations with the superintendent, he realized that they had focused on what the teachers needed but had not given enough emphasis to what principals needed to make coaching and a culture of collaboration more effective. Now the superintendent frequently asks principals about their professional-development goals and how these goals align with district vision (T. Watanabe, personal communication, August 13, 2012).

Watanabe also asks principals about their schools' professional-development goals and discusses how coaching can support them. She encourages principals to take the lead in shaping coaching at their schools. She is there to provide them with support, but principals are the ones who define what kind of support they need. In the past, Watanabe has provided elementary school principals with information about iPad apps that support the Common Core State Standards or 21st-century skills. She has shared plans for a Make-Take-Share workshop that principals could lead in their schools. In these workshops, small faculty groups create learning activities and share what they created, what students would learn, and how they would introduce the activity to students. And at the start of the school year, she asks principals if they are interested in learning more about blogging, projects with global connections, or project-based learning. If they have an interest, Watanabe is there to provide support (T. Watanabe, personal communication, August 13, 2012).

Watanabe has also worked to build the collective capacity of the district by creating a community for all the district's coaches and encouraging them to collaborate. On professional-development days when coaches can be released from schools, Watanabe brings all of them together. She may lead training on communication or collaboration skills, pedagogy, or different roles that coaches could play. Or she might sponsor a brief "un-conference." In this model, she asks coaches to share briefly about some aspect of their coaching activities. After hearing about their colleagues' work, coaches choose which of the presenters they want to meet with to learn more. Since face-to-face meetings for all coaches are rare, Watanabe also uses online tools to build community and capacity. For example, she blogs about what she learned visiting schools. One of these blogs focused on several classroom examples of how iPads were used to support literacy goals and promote 21st-century learning. As part of the blog, she asks coaches to comment on how they might use these ideas. Coaches are becoming more and more comfortable sharing their ideas online, and some coaches are beginning to write their own professional blogs to share their work with the coaching community (T. Watanabe, personal communication, August 13, 2012).

Summary

Whether implementing coaching at a school or district level, there are some common threads to success. First and foremost, educators across the school or district need to understand that coaching is an investment in educators and the school's capacity to improve teaching and learning. Building that understanding will result from:

- Regular communication about coaching between the coach, school leaders, and other educators at the school
- Expanding the scope of coaching by adding more coaches and collaborating teachers
- Coaches who, with the support of their principal, help the school adopt and act on a norm for effective learning
- Utilizing coaches and their skills in the school's professional learning communities
- School and district leadership that provides instructional leadership and resources essential to support coaching, build collective capacity to improve teaching and learning, and a culture of collaboration

FINAL THOUGHTS

Early in this book, I argued that the external-accountability model that is at the heart of the No Child Left Behind legislation had failed. As many educational researchers have argued, high-stakes testing makes teachers accountable, but schools have not offered teachers clear directions for what they should do and the support essential to ensure teachers know how to do it. I have seen a much more effective model of accountability emerge in working with Peer Coaches. In schools with effective Peer Coaches, educators have assumed a collective responsibility for their students' learning and are committed to holding each other accountable to reach this goal. One of the keys to this kind of accountability is the educators' willingness to support others to continuously improve teaching and learning. Researchers have observed the same type of collective responsibility taking place in successful schools. This body of research describes successful schools as those that have developed a culture of collaboration that is focused on improving student learning, and the school's educators are accountable to one another for continuous improvement (Barber & Mourshed, 2007; Elmore, 2004; Fullan, 2011b).

Developing this kind of collaborative culture, Fullan (2011b) argues, requires "a new role for principal as lead learner and supporter; the identification of lead teachers to play a supportive and collaborative role among peers" (p. 38). In other words, it requires individuals to serve as catalysts to unlock the power of collaboration. Peer Coaches are catalysts. Working closely with their schools' principals, Peer Coaches have demonstrated they can help schools create a culture of collaboration. They can help develop a commitment to internal accountability focused on improving teaching and learning. The coaches' role in this process is to develop the essential building blocks, including:

- Collaboration among teachers based on mutual respect and trust
- Support for educators that is friendly, private, personalized, supportive, and manageable
- Commitment to norms for collaboration that hold teachers individually and collectively accountable to improve teaching and learning

- Responsibility to improve teaching and learning by striving to implement a norm for effective learning that educators have explicitly agreed on
- Acting on the understanding that improving teaching and learning requires a commitment to a continuous process of improvement

Coaches not only help their school create this foundation for improving learning; in a sense, the coaches embody the building blocks just described. Their actions model the behaviors that shape each of the building blocks. The foundation they create, something we also have referred to as a safety net for teachers, is critical to encourage teachers to take risks and innovate. With the safety net in place, teachers are willing to take their first steps, often small steps, toward innovation. These initial successes teachers have with their students in their classrooms are critical to their buy-in to new visions for learning. And they are essential to developing those teachers' willingness to continue to take the next steps toward implementing a new vision for learning.

Wishful thinking doesn't produce the kind of innovation that improves student learning. Innovation requires a catalyst—a Peer Coach—that can help unlock the power of collaboration to improve teaching and learning.

References

ALPS. (n.d.). *Teaching for understanding.* Retrieved from http://learnweb.harvard.edu/alps/tfu/

Armstrong, A. (2012a). The art of feedback. *The Learning System, 7*(4), 1, 4–5.

Armstrong, A. (2012b). Key drivers fuel international successes. *The Learning System, 7*(2), 1, 4–5.

Barber, M., & Mourshed, M. (2007). *How the world's best-performing school systems come out on top.* Retrieved from http://mckinseyonsociety.com/how-the-worlds-best-performing-schools-come-out-on-top/

Bransford, J. D., Brown, A. L., & Cocking, R. R. (Eds.). (2000). *How people learn: Brain, mind, experience, and school.* Washington DC: National Academy Press.

Bransford, J., & Darling-Hammond, L. (Eds.). (2005). *Preparing teachers for a changing world.* San Francisco, CA: Wiley.

Chappuis, S., & Chappuis, J. (2007/2008). *The best value in formative assessment.* Retrieved from http://www.ascd.org/publications/educational-leadership/dec07/vol65/num04/The-Best-Value-in-Formative-Assessment.aspx

City, E., Elmore, R., Friarman, S., & Teitel, L. (2009). *Instructional rounds in education.* Cambridge, MA: Harvard Education Press.

Clifford, P., & Friesen, S. (2007). *Creating essential questions.* Retrieved from http://www.galileo.org/tips/essential_questions.html

Coalition of Essential Schools. (n.d.). *Essential questions.* Retrieved from http://www.essentialschools.org/benchmarks/8

Cohen, C., & Patterson, D. (2006). *T2CI evaluation findings.* Seattle, WA: Cohen Research and Evaluation.

Common Core State Standards Initiative. (2011). *English language arts standards.* Retrieved from http://www.corestandards.org/assets/CCSSI_ELA%20Standards.pdf

Covey, S. (2004). *The 7 habits of highly effective people.* New York, NY: Free Press.

Curriculum by AES. (n.d.) *Wows and wonders protocol.* Retrieved from http://curriculum.aes.ac.in/wp-content/uploads/2011/10/Wow-and-Wonder-Protocol.pdf

Darling-Hammond, L., Wei, R., Andree, A., Richardson, N., & Orphanos, S. (2009). *Professional learning in the learning profession: A status report on teacher development in the United States and abroad.* Retrieved from http://www.learningforward.org/docs/pdf/nsdcstudy2009.pdf

Dodge, J. (2009). *What are formative assessments and why should we use them?* Retrieved from http://www.scholastic.com/teachers/article/what-are-formative-assessments-and-why-should-we-use-them

Dowd, J., & D'Anieri, J. (n.d.). *Probing question exercise.* Retrieved from http://www.nsrfharmony.org/protocol/doc/probing_questions.pdf

Educational Testing Service. (2006). *2006 ICT literacy assessment preliminary findings.* Retrieved from http://www.ets.org/Media/Products/ICT_Literacy/pdf/2006_Preliminary_Findings.pdf

Elmore, R. (2004). *School reform from the inside out.* Cambridge, MA: Harvard Education Press.

Fullan, M. (2001). *Leading in a culture of change.* San Francisco, CA: Jossey-Bass.

Fullan, M. (2008). *The six secrets of change.* San Francisco, CA: Jossey-Bass.

Fullan, M. (2011a). Choosing the wrong drivers for whole school reform. *Seminar Series 204.* Retrieved from http://www.michaelfullan.ca/media/13436787590.html

Fullan, M. (2011b). *Whole system reform for innovative teaching and learning.* Retrieved from http://www.itlresearch.com/images/stories/reports/ITL%20Research%202011%20Findings%20and%20Implications%20-%20Final.pdf

Fullan, M., & Hargreaves, A. (2012). *Professional capital: Transforming teaching in every school.* New York, NY: Teachers College Press.

Furger, R. (2002). *Take a deeper look at assessment for understanding.* Retrieved from http://www.edutopia.org/performance-assessment-math

Garmston, R. (2005). Group wise: How to turn conflict into an effective learning process. *Journal of Staff Development, 26*(3).

Garmston, R., & Wellman, B. (1999). *The adaptive school: A sourcebook for developing collaborative groups.* Norwood, MA: Christopher-Gordon.

Gawande, A. (2011, October 3). Personal best: Top athletes and singers have coaches. Should you? *The New Yorker*. Retrieved from http://www.newyorker.com/reporting/2011/10/03/111003fa_fact_gawande

Gross Cheliotes, L., & Reilly, M. (2010). *Coaching conversations: Transforming your school, one conversation at a time.* Thousand Oaks, CA: Corwin.

Hanfling, S. (2011). *Peer coaching for technology integration: Evaluation report.* Helena, MT: Montana Office of Public Instruction.

Hargreaves, D. (2003). *Education epidemic: Transforming secondary schools through innovation networks.* London, UK: Demos.

Huston, M., & King-George, S. (2010). *Peer coaching: Creating a culture of collaboration worldwide.* Retrieved from http://peercoach.wordpress.com/2010/11/04/peer-coaching-creating-a-culture-of-collaboration-worldwide/

ISTE. (2007). *National educational technology standards for students, NETS•S.* Retrieved from http://www.iste.org/docs/pdfs/nets-s-standards.pdf?sfvrsn=2

ISTE. (2011). *National education technology standards for coaches, NETS•C.* Retrieved from http://www.iste.org/docs/pdfs/nets-c.pdf?sfvrsn=2

Joyce, B., & Showers, B. (1994). *Student achievement through staff development.* New York, NY: Longman.

Joyce, B., & Showers, B. (2002). *Student achievement through staff development* (3rd ed.). Alexandria, VA: Association for Supervision and Curriculum Development.

Judge, P. (Ed.). (2000). An Indian physicist puts a PC with high speed internet connection in a wall in the slums and watches what happens. *Business Week Online Daily Briefing.* Retrieved from http://www.greenstar.org/butterflies/Hole-in-the-Wall.htm

Jukes, I. (2008). *Closing the digital divide: 7 things education and educators need to do.* Retrieved from http://valleystream30.com/Assets/Technology_Documents/ctdd.pdf

Kay, K., & Greenhill, V. (2012). *The leader's guide to 21st-century education.* Upper Saddle River, NJ: Pearson Education.

Kise, J. (2012). Give teams a running start. *Journal of Staff Development, 33*(3), 38–42.

Knight, J. (2011a). *Unmistakable impact: A partnership approach for dramatically improving instruction.* Thousand Oaks, CA: Corwin.

Knight, J. (2011b). What good coaches do. *Educational Leadership, 69*(2), pp. 18–22.

Knight, J., Bradley, B., Hock, M., Skrtic, T., Knight, D., Brasseur-Hock, I., . . . Hatton, C. (2012). Record, replay, reflect: Videotaped lessons accelerate learning for teachers and coaches. *Journal of Staff Development, 33*(2), 18–23.

Kruse, S., Louis, J. S., & Bryk, A. (1994). *Building professional community in schools: Issues in restructuring schools* (Issue Report 6). Madison: University of Wisconsin, School of Education.

Ley, M. L. (2011). *Coaching and communications skills.* Retrieved from http://bit.ly/qxQiPR (now defunct)

Liston, C., Peterson, K., & Ragan, V. (2008). *Enhanced peer coaching program in Washington State: Final evaluation report.* Bothell, WA: Puget Sound Center for Teaching Learning and Technology.

Liston, C., & Ragan, V. (2009). *Enhanced peer coaching program in Washington State 2008–2009: Evaluation report.* Retrieved from http://www.k12.wa.us/EdTech/Grants/Competitive/PeerCoaching/pubdocs/PeerCoachingFinalEvaluationReport08-09.pdf

Liston, C., & Ragan, V. (2010). *Enhanced peer coaching program 2009–2010 evaluation report.* Retrieved from http://www.k12.wa.us/EdTech/Grants/Competitive/PeerCoaching/pubdocs/PeerCoachingEvaluationReport2009-10.pdf

MacDonald, E. (2011). When nice won't suffice. *Journal of Staff Development, 32*(3), 45–47.

Markow, D., & Pieters, A. (2010). *The Met Life survey of the American teacher: Collaborating for student success.* Retrieved from http://www.eric.ed.gov/PDFS/ED509650.pdf

Meyer, K., Peterson, K., McMann, M., King-George, S., Ragan, V., Huston, M., & Foltos, L. (2011a). Assess lesson design. *Peer Coaching V4.* Retrieved from http://moodle.peer-ed.com/moodle/mod/lesson/view.php?id=418 (login required)

Meyer, K., Peterson, K., McMann, M., King-George, S., Ragan, V., Huston, M., & Foltos, L. (2011b). Assessment plan. *Peer Coaching V4.* Retrieved from http://moodle.peer-ed.com/moodle/mod/lesson/view.php?id=423&pageid=140 (login required)

Meyer, K., Peterson, K., McMann, M., King-George, S., Ragan, V., Huston, M., & Foltos, L. (2011c). Coach attributes. *Peer Coaching V4.* Retrieved from http://moodle.peer-ed.com/moodle/mod/lesson/view.php?id=405 (login required)

Meyer, K., Peterson, K., McMann, M., King-George, S., Ragan, V., Huston, M., & Foltos, L. (2011d). Coach roles and responsibilities. *Peer Coaching V4.* Retrieved from http://moodle.peer-ed.com/moodle/mod/lesson/view.php?id=407&pageid=108 (login required)

Meyer, K., Peterson, K., McMann, M., King-George, S., Ragan, V., Huston, M., & Foltos, L. (2011e). Coaching cycle. *Peer Coaching V4.* Retrieved from http://moodle.peer-ed.com/moodle/mod/lesson/view.php?id=405&pageid=103 (login required)

Meyer, K., Peterson, K., McMann, M., King-George, S., Ragan, V., Huston, M., & Foltos, L. (2011f). Coaching plan. *Peer Coaching V4.* Retrieved from http://moodle.peer-ed.com/moodle/mod/lesson/view.php?id=406&pageid=106 (login required)

Meyer, K., Peterson, K., McMann, M., King-George, S., Ragan, V., Huston, M., & Foltos, L. (2011g). Coaching portfolio: Collaboration log. *Peer Coaching V4.* Retrieved from http://moodle.peer-ed.com/moodle/mod/lesson/view.php?id=413 (login required)

Meyer, K., Peterson, K., McMann, M., King-George, S., Ragan, V., Huston, M., & Foltos, L. (2011h). Coaching roadblocks. *Peer Coaching V4.* Retrieved from http://moodle.peer-ed.com/moodle/mod/lesson/view.php?id=435 (login required)

Meyer, K., Peterson, K., McMann, M., King-George, S., Ragan, V., Huston, M., & Foltos, L. (2011i). Conduct a planning meeting. *Peer Coaching V4.* Retrieved from http://moodle.peer-ed.com/moodle/mod/lesson/view.php?id=412 (login required)

Meyer, K., Peterson, K., McMann, M., King-George, S., Ragan, V., Huston, M., & Foltos, L. (2011j). Developing a task. *Peer Coaching V4.* Retrieved from http://moodle.peer-ed.com/moodle/mod/lesson/view.php?id=423&pageid=135 (login required)

Meyer, K., Peterson, K., McMann, M., King-George, S., Ragan, V., Huston, M., & Foltos, L. (2011k). Explore communications skills. *Peer Coaching V4.* Retrieved from http://moodle.peer-ed.com/moodle/mod/lesson/view.php?id=411 (login required)

Meyer, K., Peterson, K., McMann, M., King-George, S., Ragan, V., Huston, M., & Foltos, L. (2011l). Explore professional development standards. *Peer Coaching V4.* Retrieved from http://moodle.peer-ed.com/moodle/mod/lesson/view.php?id=439 (login required)

Meyer, K., Peterson, K., McMann, M., King-George, S., Ragan, V., Huston, M., & Foltos, L. (2011m). Identifying standards. *Peer Coaching V4.* Retrieved from http://moodle.peer-ed.com/moodle/mod/lesson/view.php?id=423&pageid=136 (login required)

Meyer, K., Peterson, K., McMann, M., King-George, S., Ragan, V., Huston, M., & Foltos, L. (2011n). Learning activity checklist. *Peer Coaching V4.* Retrieved from http://moodle.peer-ed.com/moodle/mod/lesson/view.php?id=417 (login required)

Meyer, K., Peterson, K., McMann, M., King-George, S., Ragan, V., Huston, M., & Foltos, L. (2011o). Learning context. *Peer Coaching V4.* Retrieved from http://moodle.peer-ed.com/moodle/mod/lesson/view.php?id=423 (login required)

Meyer, K., Peterson, K., McMann, M., King-George, S., Ragan, V., Huston, M., & Foltos, L. (2011p). Lesson improvement process: Integrating technology. *Peer Coaching V4.* Retrieved from http://moodle.peer-ed.com/moodle/mod/lesson/view .php?id=423&pageid=138 (login required)

Meyer, K., Peterson, K., McMann, M., King-George, S., Ragan, V., Huston, M., & Foltos, L. (2011q). Lesson improvement template. *Peer Coaching V4*. Retrieved from http://moodle.peer-ed.com/ moodle/mod/lesson/view.php?id=423 (login required)

Meyer, K., Peterson, K., McMann, M., King-George, S., Ragan, V., Huston, M., & Foltos, L. (2011r). Norms. *Peer Coaching V4*. Retrieved from http://moodle.peer-ed.com/moodle/mod/lesson/view .php?id=409&pageid=111 (login required)

Meyer, K., Peterson, K., McMann, M., King-George, S., Ragan, V., Huston, M., & Foltos, L. (2011s). Preparing coaches. *Peer Coaching V4*. Retrieved from http://moodle.peer-ed.com/moodle/mod/ lesson/view.php?id=407 (login required)

Meyer, K., Peterson, K., McMann, M., King-George, S., Ragan, V., Huston, M., & Foltos, L. (2011t). Program at a glance. *Peer Coaching V4*. Retrieved from http://moodle.peer-ed.com/moodle/mod/ lesson/view.php?id=407&pageid=108 (login required)

Meyer, K., Peterson, K., McMann, M., King-George, S., Ragan, V., Huston, M., & Foltos, L. (2011u). Promising practices. *Peer Coaching V4*. Retrieved from http://moodle.peer-ed.com/moodle/mod/ lesson/view.php?id=417 (login required)

Meyer, K., Peterson, K., McMann, M., King-George, S., Ragan, V., Huston, M., & Foltos, L. (2011v). Reflection and feedback. *Peer Coaching V4*. Retrieved from http://moodle.peer-ed.com/moodle/ mod/lesson/view.php?id=423&pageid=139 (login required)

Meyer, K., Peterson, K., McMann, M., King-George, S., Ragan, V., Huston, M., & Foltos, L. (2011w). Reflection on roles and trust: Building blocks of trust. *Peer Coaching V4*. Retrieved from http://moodle.peer-ed.com/moodle/mod/lesson/view .php?id=433&pageid=155 (login required)

Meyer, K., Peterson, K., McMann, M., King-George, S., Ragan, V., Huston, M., & Foltos, L. (2011x). Student directions. *Peer Coaching V4*. Retrieved from http://moodle.peer-ed.com/moodle/mod/ lesson/view.php?id=423&pageid=137 (login required)

Meyer, K., Peterson, K., McMann, M., King-George, S., Ragan, V., Huston, M., & Foltos, L. (2011y). What's working? *Peer Coaching V4*. Retrieved from http://moodle.peer-ed.com/moodle/mod/ lesson/view.php?id=441 (login required)

Meyer, K., Peterson, K., McMann, M., King-George, S., Ragan, V., Huston, M., & Foltos, L. (2011z). Why peer coaching: Type of training/classroom application. *Peer Coaching V4*. Retrieved from http://moodle.peer-ed.com/moodle/mod/lesson/view .php?id=404&pageid=100 (login required)

Meyer, K., Peterson, K., McMann, M., King-George, S., Ragan, V., Huston, M., & Foltos, L. (2011aa). Wows and wonders. *Peer Coaching V4*. Retrieved from http://moodle.peer-ed.com/moodle/mod/lesson/view.php?id=434 (login required)

Mirel, J., & Goldin, S. (2012, April 17). Alone in the classroom: Why teachers are too isolated. *The Atlantic*. Retrieved from http://www.theatlantic.com/national/archive/2012/04/alone-in-the-classroom-why-teachers-are-too-isolated/255976/

Mourshed, M., Chinezi, C., & Barber, M. (2010). *How the world's most improved school systems keep getting better*. Retrieved from http://mckinseyonsociety.com/downloads/reports/Education/How-the-Worlds-Most-Improved-School-Systems-Keep-Getting-Better_Download-version_Final.pdf

Mulford, B. (2003). The role of school leadership in attracting and retaining teachers and promoting innovative schools and students. *Review of Teaching and Teacher Education*. Canberra, Australia: Department of Education, Science and Training.

National Education Association. (2008). *Access, adequacy and equity in educational technology*. Retrieved from http://www.edutopia.org/files/existing/pdfs/NEA-Access,Adequacy,andEquityinEdTech.pdf

National School Reform Faculty. (n.d.). *Success analysis protocol for individuals*. Retrieved from http://www.nsrfharmony.org/protocol/doc/success_ana_individuals.pdf

Partnership for 21st Century Skills. (n.d.). *Framework for 21st century learning*. Retrieved from http://www.p21.org/overview

PLANE. (n.d.). *Pathways for learning anywhere, anytime—A network for educators*. Retrieved from http://my.plane.edu.au/?wantsurl=%2Flanding

Richards, A. (2003). *Making our own road: The emergence of school-based staff developers in America's public schools*. New York, NY: Edna McConnell Clark Foundation.

Richtel, M. (2011, September 3). In classroom of future, stagnant test scores. *New York Times*. Retrieved from http://www.nytimes.com/2011/09/04/technology/technology-in-schools-faces-questions-on-value.html?pagewanted=all

Rischard, J. F. (2002). *High noon: 20 global challenges, 20 years to solve them*. New York, NY: Basic Books.

Robinson, K. (2010). *RSA animate: Changing education paradigms*. Retrieved from http://www.youtube.com/watch?v=zDZFcDGpL4U

Shaw, L. (2011, February 10). In the classroom: Classroom tours aim to find great teaching. *Seattle Times*. Retrieved from http://seattletimes.com/html/localnews/2014178697_instructionalrounds10m.html

Showers, B., Murphy, C., & Joyce, B. (1996). The River City program: Staff development becomes school improvement. In B. Joyce & E. Calhoun (Eds.), *Learning experiences in school renewal: An exploration of five successful programs* (pp. 13–51). Eugene, OR: ERIC Clearinghouse on Educational Management. (ERIC Document Reproduction Services No. ED401600)

Siegler, M. G. (2010). *Eric Schmidt: Every day we create as much information as we did up to 2003.* Retrieved from http://techcrunch.com/2010/08/04/schmidt-data/

Speak Up 2007 for Students, Teachers, Parents & School Leaders. (2008). *Selected national findings: 21st century students deserve a 21st century education.* Retrieved from http://www.tomorrow.org/docs/National%20Findings%20Speak%20Up%202007.pdf

Thompson-Grove, G., Frazer, E., & Dunne, F. (n.d.). *Pocket guide to probing questions.* Retrieved from http://www.nsrfharmony.org/protocol/doc/probing_questions_guide.pdf

Tolisano, S. (2009). *Never was about technology? Time to focus on learning?* Retrieved from http://langwitches.org/blog/2009/06/17/never-was-about-technology-time-to-focus-on-learning/

Tschannen-Moran, B., & Tschannen-Moran, M. (2011). The coach and the evaluator. *Educational Leadership, 69*(2), 10–16.

van den Berg, R., Vandenberghe, R., & Sleegers, P. (1999). Management of innovations from a cultural-individual perspective. *School Effectiveness and School Improvement, 10,* 321–351.

Watanabe, T. (2011). *10 peer coaching tips in ten minutes at ISTE.* Retrieved from http://wwwatanabe.blogspot.com/2011/06/10-peer-coaching-tips-in-10-minutes-at.html

Wenglinsky, H. (1998). *Does it compute? The relationship between educational technology and student achievement in mathematics.* Retrieved from http://www.ets.org/Media/Research/pdf/PICTECHNOLOG.pdf

Wentworth, M. (2001). *Zones of comfort, risk and danger: Constructing your zone map.* Retrieved from http://www.nsrfharmony.org/protocol/doc/zones_of_comfort.pdf

Wentworth, M. (n.d.). *Chalk talk protocol.* Retrieved from http://www.nsrfharmony.org/protocol/doc/chalk_talk.pdf

Wiggins. G. (2007). What is an essential question? *Big Ideas.* Retrieved from http://www.authenticeducation.org/ae_bigideas/article.lasso?artid=53

Wurtzel, J. (2007). The professional, personified. *Journal of Staff Development, 28*(4), 30–35. Retrieved from http://www.learningforward.org/docs/jsd-fall-2007/wurtzel284.pdf?sfvrsn=2

Index

Academic focus, 61, 62 (figure)
Accountability, 82–83, 187–188
Active listening, 83–84
Advocacy, inquiry over, 87
Albert, J., 95
Altruism, 42–43
Amazon.com, 1
American Federation of Teachers, 138
Andree, A., 6, 7, 26, 49, 68, 158
Apache Junction School District, 184–187
Apple, 138
Arizona Technology in Education Association, 13, 166, 184
Armstrong, A., 104, 146
Art of Feedback, The, 104
Assessment, 129–131

Barber, M., 24–25, 30, 32, 82, 181
Bernadelli, A., 11, 19, 93
Best Value in Formative Assessment, The, 130
Bottom-up reform, 181
Bradley, B., 162
Bransford, J. D., 39, 48, 50, 89, 102
  on lesson improvement, 122, 125, 126, 129–130
Brasseur-Hock, I., 162
Brooks, S., 89

Brown, A. L., 39, 89, 102
  on lesson improvement, 122, 125, 126, 129–130
Bryk, A., 175
Building Blocks of Trust, 17
Building capacity. *See* Capacity building
Building Professional Community in Schools, 175

Calsyn, T., 4, 91–93
Capacity building, 15, 57, 73–76, 169–170
  building support for, 172–175
  implementing peer coaching and, 170–172
  to improve teaching and learning and build support, 176–180
  school leadership and, 172–174
Cator, K., 140, 141, 143
Chalk Talk, 106
Change, 23–24
Chappuis, J., 130
Chappuis, S., 130
Chinezi, C., 82
City, E., 90, 103, 158–159, 160, 163
Clarifying questions, 85
Clark, J., 162
Cleaves, P., 72, 73–74, 87, 94

Clifford, P., 123
"Closing the Digital Divide: 7
    Things Education & Educators
    Need to Do," 134
Coaching. *See* Peer coaching
Coaching Conversations, 163
Coaching Cycle, 12–13
Cocking, R. R., 39, 89, 102
    on lesson improvement, 122, 125,
        126, 129–130
Cohen, C., 68
Collaboration, 6–7, 21, 39–40
    coaching plan and, 61–65
    and communication skills, 45–47
    effective professional development
        and, 29–30, 78–79
    enhanced peer coaching with, 36
    to improve learning, 156–158
    logs, 69, 70 (figure)
    meeting norms, 79–81
    norms, 81–83, 161–162
    in peer coach training, 53
    resources, 66–68
    ripple effect and, 34–35
    safety nets for, 93
    skill development, 88–89
    structured, taught, and learned,
        79–83
    team teaching, 5, 67
    technology supporting, 136
Common Core State Standards, 3,
    124, 183, 186
Common Core State Standards
    Initiative, 50
Communication
    about coaching, 174
    active listening and, 83–84
    clarifying questions and, 85
    collaboration and, 45–47
    collaboration logs and, 69, 70
        (figure)
    inquiry over advocacy and, 87
    paraphrasing and, 84–85

in peer coaching plans, 68–71
    planning meetings, 88–89
    probing questions and, 85–87
    skill development, 88–89
    skills for peer coaches, 45–47,
        68–71, 83–87
    technology supporting, 136
Content-specific training for peer
    coaches, 51–52
Context, learning, 125, 126 (table)
Continuous improvement, 93–94
Coplanning, 67
    learning activities, 5
Covey, S., 44
Culture and peer coaching, 180

D'Anieri, J., 88
Darling-Hammond, L., 6, 7, 26, 30,
    49, 50, 68, 158
Dede, C., 133, 141, 142, 143
Deforest Action, 119–120
Directions for students,
    126–128
Dodge, J., 130
Dowd, J., 88
Dublin, G., 82, 85
Dunne, F., 86

Edmonds School, 182–183
Education
    challenges of online technology
        for, 101–102
    change in, 23–24
    for a service-based economy, 1–2
    in top performing schools, 24–25
    21st century skills and, 101–104
    See also Effective learning
Educational Testing Service, 102
Edutopia, 109
Effective learning
    assessing learning design for,
        113–118
    characteristics of, 104–109

Learning Activity Checklist,
110–113
norm for, 109–113, 177–179
positive attitude and, 115–116
starting small for, 116–118
for the 21st century, 101–104
See also Education
Egg crate isolation, 7
Einstein, A., 1, 15
Elmore, R., 2, 12, 57, 82, 90, 158–159,
160, 163, 181
on effective learning, 103, 104
on professional development, 28,
31–32
Enhanced peer coaching, 35–36
Environment for coaching, 6–8, 18
Etheredge, K., 178–179
Evaluations, teacher, 6
Expert *vs.* trust, 18–20
Expression, 137

Fear Factor, 7, 8
Fear of innovation, 91–93
Feedback, 128–129, 163
Fink, S., 25–26
Flagstaff Unified School District,
183–184
Flexibility, 18
Foltos, L., 4, 5, 18, 44, 58, 61, 80, 81,
88, 106, 109, 136, 154, 155
on assessment, 129–131
on capacity building, 15
on clarifying questions, 85
on collaboration to improve
learning, 157
on creating tasks, 122
on defining standards, 124–125
on highly effective learning, 108
on inquiry over advocacy, 87
on learning context, 125
on paraphrasing, 84
on planning meetings, 89
on probing questions, 86

on professional development, 29
reflection, 33
on starting small, 116, 117
on student directions, 126–128
on successful end to coaching
process, 14
on technology use, 105, 146, 149
on trust, 16, 21
on vision building, 175
Frazer, E., 86
Friarman, S., 90, 103, 158–159,
160, 163
Friendship in the coaching
relationship, 8–10
Friesen, S., 123
Fullan, M., 24, 51, 60, 75, 101, 181
on collaborative culture, 188
on collective capacity, 169
on effective learning, 104, 177
on professional development, 28,
30–31
Furger, R., 130

Galileo Educational Network, 109
Garmston, R., 47, 77, 79
on collaborative norms, 81, 162
on communication skills,
83, 84, 85
on inquiry over advocacy, 87
Gathering information, 136–137
Gawande, A., 6, 40
Global Integrity Leadership Group
Workshop, 84
Goldin, S., 6
Google, 138
Greenhill, V., 14
Gross Cheliotes, L., 163
Grudic, R., 11
Gunning, L., 173, 180

Ham, C., 89
Hanfling, S., 47, 73
Hargraves, A., 28

Hatton, C., 162
Helplessness, learned, 15
High Noon: 20 Global Challenges, 20 Years to Solve Them, 119
Hock, M., 162
Hogan, M., 7, 64–65, 69
How People Learn, 48, 106, 109, 125
Hunt, J., 7, 23
Hunt, P., 8, 156, 176
Huston, M., 4, 5, 18, 44, 58, 61, 74, 80, 81, 88, 106, 136, 154, 155
on assessment, 129–131
on clarifying questions, 85
on collaboration to improve learning, 157
on creating tasks, 122
on defining standards, 124–125
on highly effective learning, 108
on learning context, 125
on planning meetings, 89
on probing questions, 86
on student directions, 126–128
on technology use, 105
on vision building, 175

ICT integration. *See* Technology
Industrial Revolution learning activities, 106, 107–108 (figure), 111–112 (figure)
Innovation, 89–91
removing fear of, 91–93
Inquiry over advocacy, 87
Instructional Rounds, 160
Intensive and ongoing professional development, 30–31
International Society for Technology in Education (ISTE), 125, 135, 137, 143, 161, 166
Internet4teachers.com, 138
IREAD, 183

Joseph, R., 120
Joyce, B., 26, 29–30
Judge, P., 102

Jukes, I., 134
Just-in-time training and resources, 4

Karaitiana, V., 172–173, 180
Kay, K., 14
King, L., 16
King-George, S., 4, 5, 18, 44, 58, 61, 74, 88, 106, 136, 154, 155
on assessment, 129–131
on clarifying questions, 85
on collaboration to improve learning, 157
on collaborative norms, 80, 81
on creating tasks, 122
on defining standards, 125
on highly effective learning, 108
on learning context, 125
on paraphrasing, 85
on planning meetings, 89
on probing questions, 86
on student directions, 126–128
on technology use, 105
on vision building, 175
Kise, J., 79
Knight, D., 162
Knight, J., 9, 10, 60, 64, 65, 69, 82, 162
Knight, M., 183–184
Kruse, S., 175

Learned helplessness, 15
Learning Activity Checklist, 110–113, 123, 130, 144–145, 147, 161, 176, 178
Learning context, 125, 126 (table)
Lesson design, 47–49, 113–118
Lesson improvement, 119–122
assessment, 129–131
creating a task and, 122–124
defining standards for, 124–125
learning context and, 125, 126 (table)
peer coaching technology, 150
reflection and feedback for, 128–129

resources, 131–132
student directions and, 126–128
template, 126 (table), 127–128
Ley, M. L., 36–37, 95–96, 150–151,
    159–160, 161
Linklater, J., 52, 77, 78, 88, 90, 156,
    166, 176
Listening, active, 83–84
Liston, C., 22, 35–36, 59, 66, 164
Logarithms, 1–2
Logs, collaboration, 69, 70 (figure)
Louis, J. S., 175

MacDonald, E., 89–90, 158
Macleod-Jones, D., 95, 156, 176
Manageable coaching relationships,
    11–14
Markow, D., 6
Mathey, K., 182–183
Matsuzawa, P., 34–35
McCauley, M., 74
McMann, M., 4, 5, 18, 44, 58, 61, 88,
    106, 136, 154, 155
    on assessment, 129–131
    on clarifying questions, 85
    on collaboration to improve
        learning, 157
    on collaborative norms, 80, 81
    on creating tasks, 122
    on defining standards, 124–125
    on highly effective
        learning, 108
    on learning context, 125
    on paraphrasing, 85
    on planning meetings, 89
    on probing questions, 86
    on student directions, 126–128
    on technology use, 105
    on vision building, 175
Meetings, planning, 88–89
Meyer, K., 4, 5, 18, 44, 58, 61, 88, 106,
    136, 154, 155
    on assessment, 129–131
    on clarifying questions, 85

on collaboration to improve
    learning, 157
on collaborative norms, 80, 81
on creating tasks, 122
on defining standards, 124–125
on highly effective learning, 108
on learning context, 125
on paraphrasing, 85
on planning meetings, 89
on probing questions, 86
on student directions, 126–128
on technology use, 105
on vision building, 175
Microsoft, 32, 69, 138
Mirel, J., 6
Mitra. S., 102
Modeling, 5, 67
    risk taking, 95
Mourshed, M., 24–25, 30, 32,
    82, 181
Mulford, B., 28, 60
Murphy, C., 30

National Education Association,
    138, 139
National School Reform Faculty
    (NSRF), 86, 88, 96, 106, 155, 157
NETS•C, 137
NETS•S, 135–136, 143
No Child Left Behind (NCLB), 7,
    187–188
Norms, coaching, 65–66
    collaborative, 81–83, 161–162
    for effective learning, 109–113,
        177–179
    meeting, 79–81

Observation, 5–6, 158–161
    feedback and, 163
    video and, 162
Ongoing and intensive professional
    development, 30–31, 164–167
Organization information, 137
Orphanos, S., 6, 7, 26, 49, 68, 158

Paraphrasing, 84–85
Partnership for 21st Century Skills,
    2, 124
Patterson, D., 68
Pedagogy driving technology use,
    145–146
Peer coaches, 39–40
    active listening by, 83–84
    beginning with the end in mind,
        44–45
    carrying out roles and responsi-
        bilities, 20–22, 65
    challenging probing questions,
        95–99
    classroom practice and training
        of, 53–54
    collaborative training of, 53
    communication and collaboration
        skills, 45–47, 68–71, 83–87
    content-specific training for,
        51–52
    essential knowledge for, 43–52, 46
        (figure)
    ICT integration by, 49–51
    increasing number of, 176–177
    intensive, sustained training of, 54
    learning from successes and
        challenges, 154–156
    lesson design by, 47–49
    meeting norms, 79–81
    modeling risk taking, 95
    paraphrasing by, 84–85
    professional learning communi-
        ties and, 71–72, 179–180
    recognizing teachers for work,
        94–95
    as safety nets, 93
    teachers becoming, 40–43
    technology training for, 137–138
    training, 52–54
Peer coaching
    building capacity, 15, 57, 73–76
    change through, 23–24

collaborative in Wisconsin, 36–37
communicating about, 174
culture and, 180
cycle, 12–13
defined, 3
defining the coaching relationship
    in, 8–16
effectiveness of, 34–37
effective professional learning
    and, 32–34
encouraging continuous
    improvement, 93–94
enhanced, 35–36
expense versus investment,
    171–172
feedback, 128–129, 163
focused on the learners, 158–160
friendship in, 8–10
getting started with, 3–8
goal of, 78
helping teachers integrate
    technology, 147–149
how coaches carry out roles in,
    20–22
implementing, 170–172
making the decision to implement,
    59–60
manageable relationships in,
    11–14
measuring progress of, 72–73
observation in, 5–6, 158–161
ongoing professional learning
    and, 30–31, 164–167
origins of, 3–4
personalized, 10–11
positive attitude and, 115–116
privacy, 14
protocol, 154–155
relationships, respect, and trust,
    16–22
ripple effect of, 34–35
as risk taking, 8, 18, 95
roles in, 4–6

starting small, 116–118
successful, 77–78
supportive, 14–16
as a system thing, not a single
thing, 181–187
technology integration toolkit,
149–151
understanding the environment
for, 6–8, 18
vision building and, 174–175
in Washington state, 35–36
in Wisconsin, 36–37
Personalized coaching, 10–11
Peterson, K., 4, 5, 18, 22, 35, 44, 58,
59, 61, 88, 106, 136, 154, 155
on assessment, 129–131
on clarifying questions, 85
on collaboration to improve
learning, 157
on collaborative norms, 80, 81
on creating tasks, 122
on defining standards, 124–125
on highly effective learning, 108
on learning context, 125
on paraphrasing, 85
on planning meetings, 89
on probing questions, 86
on student directions, 126–128
on technology use, 105
on vision building, 175
Pieters, A., 6
PLANE program, 166
Plans, coaching, 57–59
academic focus, 61, 62 (figure)
aligned with professional
development, 71–72
for building capacity, 73–76
coach roles and responsibilities
in, 65
collaborating teachers and, 61–63
creating, 60–61
effective communication and,
68–71

elements of, 61–73
measuring progress of, 72–73
meetings, 88–89
norms, 65–66
resources, 66–71
three model for choosing a
collaborating teacher in, 63–65
Porat, J., 63–64
Preobservation meetings, 160–161
Preparing Teachers for a Changing
World, 50
Principals, 68–70
Privacy in coaching relationship, 14
Probing questions, 85–87
challenging, 95–99
Professional development
aligned with coaching
plans, 71–72
characteristics of effective, 29–32
focus of, 26–27
highly collaborative, 29–30, 78–79
intensive, 30–31
on the job, connected to classroom
practice, 31–32
ongoing, 30–31, 164–167
peer coaching and effective, 32–34
that works, 27–29
as wishful thinking, 25–27
Professional learning communities
(PLC), 71–72, 179–180
Protocol, 154–155, 162–163

Quah, V., 171
Questions
clarifying, 85
probing, 85–87, 95–99

Race to the Top program, 7
Ragan, V., 4, 5, 18, 22, 35–36, 44, 58,
59, 61, 66, 80, 81, 88, 106, 136,
154, 155, 164
on assessment, 129–131
on clarifying questions, 85

on collaboration to improve
    learning, 157
on creating tasks, 122
on defining standards, 124–125
on highly effective
    learning, 108
on learning context, 125
on planning meetings, 89
on probing questions, 86
on student directions, 126–128
on technology use, 105
on vision building, 175
Recognition, 94–95
Record, Replay, Reflect, 162
Reeder, E., 109–110
Reflection, 5–6, 128–129
    collaborative norms and, 161–162
    protocols and, 162–163
    video and observation in, 162
Reilly, M., 163
Relationships, coaching
    friendly, 8–10
    manageable, 11–14
    personalized, 10–11
    privacy, 14
    respect and trust in, 16–22
    supportive, 14–16
Resources
    coaching plan, 66–71
    lesson improvement, 131–132
Respect, 81
Richards, A., 40, 68
Richardson, N., 6, 7, 26, 49, 158
Richtel, M., 139, 140, 143
Ripple effect, 34–35
Rischard, J. F., 119
Risk taking, 8, 18, 95
Roberts, D., 144
Roberts, P., 120
Robert's Rule, 80
Robinson, K., 1
Roles, coaching, 4–6
Ruggles, M., 162

Safety nets, 93
Schmidt, E., 101–102
School leadership, 172–174
Service-based economy, 1–2
Shanahan, P., 10, 20, 42
Shaw, L., 26
Showers, B., 26, 29–30
Siegler, M. G., 102
Skrtic T., 162
Sleegers, P., 28
Socrates, 15
Soderberg, L., 182
Soine, K., 63
Speak Up, 49–50
Standardized testing, 7, 139–141
Standards, defining, 124–125
Streeval, A., 106
Student directions and lesson
    improvement, 126–128
Supportive coaching relationships,
    14–16

*Take a Deeper Look at Assessment for
    Understanding,* 130
Taking it Global Website, 120
Task creation, 122–124, 151
Teacher(s)
    assigned to work with a coach,
        63–64
    belief about collaboration, 6
    coached to integrate technology,
        147–149
    evaluations, 6
    holding the power to improve,
        28–29
    recognition of, 94–95
    taking on the coach role, 39–40
    team teaching, 5, 67
    willing to collaborate, 63
    See also Collaboration;
        Professional development
Teaching for Understanding, 109
Team teaching, 5, 67

Technology
    aiding learning, 141–146
    coaching linking learning and,
        135–139
    coaching teachers to integrate,
        147–149
    emphasizing student tasks in us-
        ing, 151
    integration, 49–51, 133–135, 142,
        183–184
    integration as peeling the onion,
        150–151
    integration redefined, 146–149
    pedagogy driving use of, 145–146
    as Play-Doh, 141–142
    supporting and enhancing 21st-
        century learning, 143–145
    supporting collaboration, 136
    supporting communication, 136
    supporting expression, 137
    supporting gathering information,
        136–137
    supporting organizing
        information, 137
    test scores and, 139–141
    tool kit for peer coaching, 149–151
    transforming traditional teaching
        and learning, 142–143
Teitel, L., 90, 103, 158–159, 160, 163
Testing, standardized, 7, 139–141
Thompson-Grove, G., 86
Tolisano, S., 142, 145
Training of peer coaches, 52–54
Trust, 16, 21, 81
    Building Blocks of, 17
    expert *vs.*, 18–20

Tschannen-Moran, B., 116
Tschannen-Moran, M., 116

Understanding by Design, 109

Van den Berg, R., 28
Vandenberghe, R., 28
Video and observation, 162
Vision building, 174–175

Walter, A., 9, 11, 15, 43
Warmouth, J., 8, 97–99
Watanabe, T., 9, 70, 72, 94–95, 142,
        165, 177–178
    Apache Junction School District
        and, 184–187
Wei, R., 6, 7, 26, 49, 68, 158
Wellman, B., 47, 77, 79
    on collaborative norms, 81, 162
    on communication skills, 83,
        84, 85
    on inquiry over advocacy, 87
Wenglensky, H., 143
Wentworth, M., 106
*What Are Formative Assessments
        and Why Should We Use
        Them?*, 130
What Good Coaches Do, 10
What Is an Essential Question?, 123
Wiggins, G., 109, 123
Wisconsin, 36–37
Wows and Wonders, 154, 155–156
Wurtzel, J., 28

Zones of Comfort, Risk and Danger, 96

CORWIN

A SAGE Company

The Corwin logo—a raven striding across an open book—represents the union of courage and learning. Corwin is committed to improving education for all learners by publishing books and other professional development resources for those serving the field of PreK–12 education. By providing practical, hands-on materials, Corwin continues to carry out the promise of its motto: **"Helping Educators Do Their Work Better."**